ARCHITECTURE IN NEW YORK

ARCHITECTURE

IN NEW YORK

A PHOTOGRAPHIC HISTORY

WAYNE ANDREWS

SYRACUSE UNIVERSITY PRESS

Copyright © 1969, 1995 by Wayne Andrews

All Rights Reserved

First Syracuse University Press Edition 1995
95 96 97 98 99 00   6 5 4 3 2 1

The paper used in this publication meets the minimum requirements of American National Standard for Information Sciences—Permanence of Paper for Printed Library Materials, ANSI Z39.48-1984. ∞™

This edition originally published by Atheneum Books, reprinted by arrangement with Scribner, an imprint of Simon & Schuster.

Library of Congress Cataloging-in-Publication Data

Andrews, Wayne.
    Architecture in New York : a photographic history / Wayne Andrews.
      p. cm.
    Originally published: New York : Atheneum, 1969.
    Includes bibliographical references (p.   ) and index.
    ISBN 0-8156-0309-6 (pbk.)
     1. Architecture—New York (State)—Pictorial works. I. Title.
NA730.N4A7 1995
720'.9747—dc20   94-25294

Manufactured in the United States of America

CONTENTS

PHOTOGRAPHIC CREDITS AND ACKNOWLEDGMENTS

I am indebted to Brown Brothers for the portraits of Richard Morris Hunt, Stanford White and Alva Vanderbilt in the introduction, for the Astor House (44), Washington Square (52), the Jerome and Stewart mansions (62), the library of W. H. Vanderbilt (73), the W. K. Vanderbilt mansion (77), the Elbridge T. Gerry mansion (80), the living room of Mrs. William B. Astor (81), the Flatiron Building (114), the Produce Exchange (115), the New York Central Building (123), the Singer Building at 149 Broadway (127), the James Speyer mansion (136), the George J. Gould mansion (137), and the Daily News Building (157); to CBS for the CBS Building (177); to Culver Pictures Inc. for the interior of the W. K. Vanderbilt mansion (76) and that of the Cornelius Vanderbilt II mansion (78); to McGraw-Hill, Inc., for the McGraw-Hill Building (156); to the Museum of the City of New York for the Byron views of the W. H. Vanderbilt houses (72), the Cornelius Vanderbilt II mansion (79), the Mrs. William B. Astor mansion (81), and the Louis C. Tiffany house (91), as well as for New York University and the House of Mansions (30), the Eccentric Mills (61), the National Academy of Design (66), the Herald Building and Louis Sherry ballroom (94), the W. K. Vanderbilt, Jr., mansion (95), the Madison Square Presbyterian Church (100), the Joseph Pulitzer mansion (104), the interior and exterior of the Payne Whitney mansion (105), the interior and exterior of the Clarence H. Mackay mansion (106), the ballroom of William C. Whitney (107), and the two views of Madison Square Garden (110 and 111); to the Museum of Modern Art for the interior and exterior of the Larkin Administration Building (148 and 149); to the New-York Historical Society for Federal Hall (11), Saint John's Chapel and Saint John's Park (18), the John C. Stevens house and the A. J. Davis interior (32), the Cathedral of Saint John the Divine (87), and the Tiffany Building (101); to the New York Public Library for the W. H. C. Waddell house (Phelps-Stokes Collection) (31); to Richard Nickel for the cornice of the Bayard Building (146); to the Penn Central System for the interior and exterior of Grand Central (122); to Rockefeller Center for Saint Patrick's Cathedral (42) and Rockefeller Center (158); to St. Regis-Sheraton for the doorway of the St. Regis (130); to Nathan Silver for the Singer Building at 561 Broadway (128); to the Singer Company for the Singer Tower at 149 Broadway (126); to Ezra Stoller Associates (Esto) for the interior of the Pierpont Morgan Library (99) and the Seagram Building (159); and to Wildenstein & Co. for the Wildenstein Gallery (135).

All other photographs are my own.

I should also like to thank A. K. Baragwanath for his exceptional courtesy at the Museum of the City of New York and Dr. James J. Heslin of the New-York Historical Society for permitting a graduate of that institution to roam through the stacks. Nor should I forget the generosity of Mayor Erastus Corning II of Albany, Kenneth H. MacFarland, Librarian of the Albany Institute of History and Art, and Arthur B. Gregg, Town Historian of Guilderland, who helped me run down the history of the Schoolcraft house in Guiderland. And although I have already listed in the bibliography the most useful books I consulted, I should like to single out Jewel Helen Conover's *Nineteenth Century Houses in Western New York*. Her unprejudiced eyes have discovered so much in that territory that it is to be hoped other local historians will follow her example. She also had the kindness to unearth for me the Timothy Brown house at Georgetown. While I can't mention all the friends who have accompanied me on my excursions, I cannot very well forget the hospitality of Miss Elizabeth Holahan of Rochester, nor that of Quinn Smith of Warren, Pennsylvania, who drove so many miles with me in Western New York.

Acknowledgment is also made to Condé Nast Publications for permission to quote from John Jay Chapman's "McKim, Mead & White," *Vanity Fair*, September, 1919; to Harper & Row to quote from Consuelo Vanderbilt Balsan's *The Glitter and the Gold;* to Colonel James M. Moore for permission to quote from Charles Moore's *Charles Follen McKim;* and to Charles Scribner's Sons to quote from Edith Wharton's *A Backward Glance*.

My friends Alan Burnham, Leonard Eaton, Harwell Hamilton Harris and Russell Lynes were so generous as to read the first draft of the introduction.

But this book can't be published without a final word about the faithful collaboration of Richard Schuler, Ernest Pile and Sybil Collins of Compo Photo Service, who have developed and enlarged all of my negatives and given me more good advice than I deserved.

"IT IS ONLY IN NEW YORK..."

For centuries the architecture of New York City and New York State has been a matter of serious concern to earnest men and women. As early as the spring of 1785, Robert Livingston, Third Lord of the Manor, made plain to one of his children that he was "sorry to learn that living in our capital is become so very expensive, and what is worse, that it is become fashionable." The Third Lord was spared the spectacle of the nineteenth century, when the very mention of Manhattan spelled extravagance.

The word extravagance cannot be mentioned too soon, for a surprising number of famous buildings in Manhattan history give the impression they were designed for clients whose budgets were unlimited. In fact, if you were searching for the particular contribution of the city to American architecture, the palaces of the millionaires and the clubs they distinguished would come instantly to mind. This is not to be taken as a slur upon Trinity Church and the other monuments of the Greek and Gothic Revivals before the Civil War, and it would be stupid to ignore the claims of Wright's Guggenheim Museum, Saarinen's TWA Terminal and CBS tower, and other modern buildings. But the truth is that Fifth Avenue was most remarkable when it was noted, not for its apartment houses, but for its mansions.

You may protest that stopping the clock at a certain hour is no way to begin to consider the progress of Manhattan Island from the seventeenth century to our own. In any event, you will be absolutely correct if you insist that New York State as a whole defies not only this generalization but any other. The state is not a region but an uncountable collection of regions, each of which has or had the temerity to be true to itself. Henry James was aware of this when he selected Albany as the site of Isabel Archer's childhood. "I like places in which things have happened—even if they're sad things," Isabel tells Mrs. Touchett at the beginning of *The Portrait of a Lady*. And Daisy Miller's little brother Randolph pays an equally emphatic tribute to his birthplace: "My father's in Schenectady. He's got a big business. My father's rich, you bet." James would have understood that Rensselaerville could pass for a New England village, and Buffalo, where Sullivan and Wright were made welcome, for a satellite of Chicago. This wide divergence from one area to another is not without its advantages: one result is that the architecture of the state offers an excellent exhibit of every conceivable trend from the early nineteenth century to the present.

To return to Manhattan. The palaces, most of them, have been demolished, but the remaining examples are often embarrassingly beautiful to modern architects who keep their eyes open. Le Corbusier, who could well afford to entertain unconventional opinions, may have been recalling the Villard mansions by McKim, Mead & White when he wrote that "It is only in New York that I begin to appreciate the Italian Renaissance. It is so well done that you might almost believe it is the real thing."

A palace, it is hardly necessary to add, would have been inconceivable in colonial times. Affluence was a mirage on the horizon. As the will of Lewis Morris, Second Lord of the Manor of Morrisania, indicates, the better families of the eighteenth century lived in dread of the day some unscrupulous Yankee would swindle them out of their hard-earned savings. "It is my desire," Morris declared, "that my son Gouverneur Morris may have the best education that is to be had in Europe or America, but my express will and directions are that he never be sent for that purpose to the Colony of Connecticut lest he should imbibe in his youth that low craft and cunning so incident to the people of that country, which is so interwoven in their constitution that all their art cannot disguise it from the world, though many of them under the sanctified garb of religion have endeavored to impose themselves on the world as honest men."

Since the fine art of architecture depends as does no other on cash on hand and cash anticipated, it is not surprising that the colonial period offers only modest rewards for connoisseurs. Sir William Johnson may have been one of the great landowners of the Mohawk Valley, but neither Fort Johnson, Johnson Hall, nor Guy Park, the estate of his nephew, could compare with the mansions of the planters along the James or the Rappahannock. Nor was there any town house to match Miles Brewton's in Charleston. In churches too New York was disappointing. Saint Paul's Chapel on Broadway was a commendable effort to recall the distinction of Saint Martin-in-the-Fields in London, but its tower and steeple date from after the Revolution, as does the altar-screen by Pierre-Charles L'Enfant.

By 1789, however, L'Enfant transformed the old city hall into the temporary capitol of the United States. And by 1810, New York, with nearly 100,000 inhabitants, was already the nation's biggest city. Opportunities were at last available in the state. No one should overlook the prudent but charming achievements of Ephraim Russ, the carpenter-architect·of Rensselaerville. An even more significant figure was Philip Hooker of Schenectady, long a surveyor, who managed to design not only the city hall of Albany, now demolished, but also Albany Academy, the chapel of Hamilton College, and, most important of all, the rather elegant retreat at Cooperstown of the English-born landholder George Hyde Clark. Moreover, L'Enfant was not the only refugee from revolutionary Europe whose talent was manifest to New Yorkers. Joseph-Jacques Ramée, once a favorite of Louis XVI's brother the Duc d'Artois, came from exile in Copenhagen to fashion the first building of Union College and to make plans, unhappily never carried out, for the campus. Finally, there was Joseph-François Mangin, yet another Frenchman, to whom we owe the exquisite Louis XVI façade of New York City Hall. Associated with him on this commission was the American John McComb, Jr., who with his brother

Isaac gave us that evocation of Georgian London, Saint John's Chapel, around which centered Saint John's park or Hudson Square. Like the church, the park has vanished.

But it was only in 1825, when DeWitt Clinton, rejoicing in the completion of the Erie Canal he championed, led a procession of canal boats from Buffalo to New York, that the economic advantages of New York harbor and New York State were obvious. Prior to the Erie Canal, New York was envious rather than envied.

In the thirty-five years that followed Clinton's celebration, New York became—although Philadelphians may contest this—the architectural center of the nation. Thanks to the prestige of men like Alexander Jackson Davis, Andrew Jackson Downing, Minard Lafever, James Renwick, Jr., and Richard Upjohn, patrons flocked from everywhere in search of Grecian villas, Gothic cottages, and even an occasional Egyptian church. It was just as well that Lewis Morris did not live to see these things, for in this era Manhattan came close to becoming a Yankee city. "New Englanders," the historian Robert Albion has informed us, "captured New York port about 1820 and dominated its business until after the Civil War." Among those who made good were the Griswolds from Old Lyme, the Howlands from Norwich and the Grinnells from New Bedford. "He needs but a foothold," wrote an early chronicler of the Yankee on the make. "He asks no more, and he is as sure to keep it as that light will dispel darkness." Such men set the standards that attracted quick-witted bankers. They also reminded speculators of the possibilities of railroads.

It was once the fashion to smile at the endeavors of the architects of the romantic revivals that flourished in these years. We smile no longer. Conscientious historians have discovered that these revivals challenged the authority of the Renaissance and so stimulated the beginning of modern architecture.

At this, Alexander Jackson Davis would be most surprised. His taste was formed, not by lectures on the engineering of Gothic cathedrals, but by the Gothic novels spoofed by Jane Austen in *Northanger Abbey:* his diaries reveal that he never outgrew a fondness for the tales of Ann Radcliffe. In his teens he spent every spare moment sketching "some ancient castle of romance, arranging the trapdoors, subterraneous passages and drawbridges." His genius as a draftsman was evident in 1828, when at twenty-five he became the partner of Ithiel Town, a bridge-builder from New Haven who had acquired what was at the time a considerable architectural library. The partnership was brief; Davis needed no aid at the drafting table and none when it came to charming clients.

One of the most obliging of these was the merchant William Paulding, who decided in 1838 on a marble Gothic castle in Tarrytown. Mayor Philip Hone of New York, whose diary will always be consulted by those who wish to relive the romantic years, took the trouble to call at Lyndhurst, as the castle came to be known, and was made a trifle nervous by its "towers, turrets and trellises; minarets, mosaics and mouseholes; archways, armories and airholes." A greater connoisseur than he was Jay Gould, who bought the estate in 1880. Gould's touch was death, claimed one of his unhappy rivals on Wall Street. This may have been so, but he was a lively student of the Gothic Revival. Long before he planned his raids on the Erie Railroad, he earned his living designing and peddling maps. That of Albany County, meticulously illustrated with Gothic villas on the borders, is a minor but impeccable document for the history of American architecture. His daughter Anna, Duchess of Talleyrand, recently bequeathed Lyndhurst to the National Trust, and today anyone may invade the grounds and scold Hone for his myopic vision.

The Mayor was more generous to another creation of Davis, the Grecian town house in Manhattan of John Cox Stevens, who married a Livingston and founded the New York Yacht Club. "The Palais Bourbon in Paris, Buckingham Palace in London and Sans Souci in Berlin are little grander than this residence of a simple citizen of our republican city," he reported. The Stevens house is gone, which is regrettable, but Davis himself would have considered the Gothic castle of greater importance. The Gothic was his first love and his last, even though he could—and frequently did—furnish designs in *any* style, not excepting the Moorish.

Far stricter than Davis was his great friend Andrew Jackson Downing of Newburgh, the landscape artist turned critic, who launched a nationwide campaign for Gothic castles and cottages. Quite naturally he frowned on those whose taste was Grecian. "The Greek temple disease has passed its crisis," he announced in 1846. "The people have survived it." If so, he was largely responsible.

Downing was nothing if not persuasive. "There is," he observed, "something wonderfully captivating in the idea of a battlemented castle, even to an apparently modest man, who thus shows to the world his unsuspected vein of personal ambition. But, *unless there be something of the castle in the man*, it is very likely, if it be like a real castle, to dwarf him to the stature of a mouse."

Downing could also be strangely modern. Like Frank Lloyd Wright, he was fond of expressing the nature of materials. "When we employ stone as a building material, let it be clearly expressed," he advised. "When we employ wood, there should be no less frankness in avowing the material." Wrightian too was his reverence for the site, and it could be argued that the informal, assymetrical houses in his books marked an advance toward the open planning of our age.

A gardener's son, Downing made a most aristocratic impression on those who were permitted to pay their respects at his (now leveled) Gothic home at Newburgh. His was "the easy elegance and perfect savoir-faire which would have adorned the Escorial," one guest testified. Which makes his great concern for a public park in Manhattan all the more unusual. He and William Cullen Bryant led the fight for the Central Park laid out by Frederick Law Olmsted in 1857. "Social doubters," Downing insisted when the complaint was made that the enjoyment of nature was beyond the average man, "mistake our people and our destiny. If we would but listen to them, our magnificent river and lake steamers, those real palaces of the millions, would have had no velvet couches, no splendid mirrors, no luxurious carpets. . . . And yet . . . are they not respected by the majority who use them, as truly as other palaces by their rightful sovereigns?"

Downing died a hero's death in 1852 in a steamboat disaster on the Hudson, but not before he saluted Richard Upjohn for the design of Trinity

Church. This major monument of the Gothic Revival in America owes much to the architect's study of Pugin's work in England but even more to his own respect for high churchmanship. "The object," said Upjohn, "is not to surprise with novelties in church architecture, but to make what is to be made truly ecclesiastical—a temple of solemnities—such as will fix the attention of persons, and make them respond in heart and spirit to the opening service: *The Lord is in His Holy Temple, let all the earth keep silence.*" There was no doubting Upjohn's faith in the Episcopal Church, nor his success at Trinity, Ascension and the Church of the Holy Communion. However, when not planning for his fellow Anglicans, he could be ill at ease. He declined doing a church for the Unitarians of Boston, even though a tolerant Episcopalian pleaded that nowhere was there a class of men "whose private life is more pure." When he did design a Presbyterian church, his misgivings were apparent to another architect, who decided that "he did it conscientiously, upon the ground that Presbyterians were not entitled to architecture."

Upjohn's great rival in the ecclesiastical domain, James Renwick, Jr., was a more worldly artist who kept two steam yachts, one for fishing off the Florida coast, the other for more ambitious destinations. Although an Episcopalian, he had no objection to creating Saint Patrick's Cathedral for the Romans. His masterpiece, however, was Grace Church on Broadway, which he completed in 1846 when only twenty-eight. "This is to be the fashionable church," conceded Philip Hone, himself a vestryman of Trinity. Sexton Isaac Brown of Grace was to prove worthy of this advertisement. The Lenten Season was "horridly dull," he confessed, but then "we make our funerals as entertaining as possible."

No such frivolity is attached to any of the buildings of Minard Lafever, who began life as a carpenter in the Finger Lakes. The author of remarkable manuals for carpenters and builders, he labored with admirable patience over the details of his great Gothic church, Holy Trinity on Brooklyn Heights. He was a master, as well, of the Greek and Egyptian Revivals, and to him have been attributed the

Hunting house and the Whalers' Church at Sag Harbor.

So much for the most famous names of the early nineteenth century. To list their achievements is only to begin to explore the delights of the romantic revivals. There were carpenters in those days whose names have been forgotten but whose intransigent individuality is more than welcome to twentieth-century eyes. One such artisan was the man who sawed the aggressively Gothic bargeboards for the gate lodge of Gardiner Howland at New Hamburgh near Poughkeepsie. There were also amateurs who knew how to express frantic desires with fascinating skill. One of these was the spiritualist Timothy Brown of Georgetown near Cazenovia, who with ax, saw, jack-knife and drawshave built a rather Moorish villa all his own toward 1850.

In the meantime James Bogardus, who erected the first cast-iron building in 1848, was prophesying the steel frames of the skyscrapers of our age. "Such a building," said Bogardus of his invention, "may be erected with extraordinary facility and at all seasons of the year. No plumb is needed, no square, no level. As fast as the pieces may be handled, they may be adjusted and secured by the most ignorant workman; the building cannot fail to be both perpendicular and firm."

The skyscraper drew even nearer in 1857 when Elijah Otis installed the first practical passenger elevator in the cast-iron Haughwout Building at 488 Broadway. A year later an enthusiastic young designer by the name of Henry Van Brunt read a most startling paper on cast iron before a New York meeting of the American Institute of Architects, trying the tempers of revivalists who failed to hail the new material. "This is an iron age," Van Brunt lectured his colleagues. "But architecture, sitting haughtily on her acropolis, has indignantly refused to receive it, or receiving it, has done so stealthily and unworthily, enslaving it to basest uses, and denying honor and grace to its toil." This Ruskinian sermon did not please Leopold Eidlitz, the very man who fathomed the mind of Upjohn when confronted with the commission for a Presbyterian church. Iron, Eidlitz was so unkind as to remind

Van Brunt, was a combustible material: it could melt. Which was quite true, as a series of disastrous fires was to demonstrate.

Van Brunt may have been a prophet, but the future of architecture is not invariably decided by the opinions of high-minded young men. In the quarter century following his speech, a most glorious confusion raged in the profession, not only in New York but everywhere. The Grecian villages and Gothic cottages of the 1830s, '40s and '50s seemed strangely old-fashioned, and the argument was violent over what should take their place. There were disciples of Ruskin, like Peter Bonnett Wight, the contriver of the National Academy of Design that once stood on the corner of Fourth Avenue and Twenty-third Street, who fancied that the Venetian Gothic endorsed by the master was the only answer. The Ruskinians are not to be laughed at: the faithful readers of *The Stones of Venice* may be counted, some of them, among the pioneers of modern architecture, and J. L. Silsbee, the architect of the most Ruskinian Syracuse Savings Bank, no sooner moved to Chicago than he gave Frank Lloyd Wright his first job.

But Wight and Silsbee were contradicted on every side by those who imagined that the mansard roofs so prominent in the Paris of the Second Empire should crown every village from coast to coast. The mansardic style had been introduced to Fifth Avenue in 1851, a year before Napoleon III's coup d'état. It won greater prestige in 1865 when Renwick displayed its pomp and circumstance at Vassar. In 1872 it scored another victory at Saratoga with the completion of the Grand Union Hotel.

You might label this the Age of Indecision, for it will not fall into any particular pattern. But if America had not yet made up its mind, it saw no reason to be modest, and the magnificently brazen vulgarity of the Grand Union (pulled down for no good reason twenty years ago) proved that the American people could not accept meek solutions. There was certainly nothing meek about Olana, the princely villa five miles south of the town of Hudson where the enormously successful landscape painter Frederic E. Church rested in 1874 from his labors rendering the great volcanoes of the world. Church is believed to have called on Olmsted, the creator of Central Park, for help in laying out his grounds. The task was imposing, for Olana commands the ultimate view of the Hudson Valley, stretching from the Catskills to the first hint of the Berkshires. The painter's assistant in the design of the house was Calvert Vaux, once the partner of Andrew Jackson Downing, but it is likely that this American version of Persian splendor was mainly the work of Church himself. He had traveled to the Near East in search of majestic subjects.

Olana, maintained today by the New York State Historic Trust, might be the perfect residence for an artist. The perfect home for a millionaire was not invented without soul-searching. This problem may seem academic in the late twentieth century, but it was pressing a hundred years ago, when the masters of the great fortunes cast a longer shadow than any occupant of the White House.

New York was not innocent of millionaires in the age of A. J. Davis. When the snuff manufacturer Pierre Lorillard died in 1843, he was given this new title, although he seems to have accumulated no more than *one* million. Five years later John Jacob Astor left $20,000,000. This, however, was a mere trifle compared with the $105,000,000 amassed by Commodore Cornelius Vanderbilt at his death in 1877. A summit had been reached, and no architect could ignore the fact that the late nineteenth century was destined to reflect the eminence of the multi-millionaires.

The size of the Commodore's estate must have charmed many a designer, and it is sad that no member of the profession succeeded in spending more than a fraction of the total. The creator of the New York Central System breathed his last in a quiet Greek Revival house at 10 Washington Place. Yet he was no recluse. He made believe that he played the market on tips provided by the trances of Victoria Woodhull, a champion in her time of free love and women's suffrage. He also had no hesitation about naming the best of his locomotives after himself and fixing his portrait on the lamp above the cow-catcher. Nor did he think twice before erecting a statue to himself in front of the freight station at Saint John's Park.

William Henry Vanderbilt, the Commodore's son, is usually remembered for having proclaimed "The public be damned!" when asked by a reporter whether he ran trains to Chicago for the public's benefit, but this was not his only achievement. He turned the $90,000,000 he inherited into $200,000,000 before his death in 1885, and he was tempted—if not seduced—by the art of architecture. He hired John B. Snook, planner of the first Grand Central Station, and the decorating firm of Herter Brothers to do their very best with three huge mansions on the west side of Fifth Avenue between Fifty-first and Fifty-second Streets for himself and two of his daughters. Snook was doubtless enchanted by the commission. His disappointment came when he found that Vanderbilt shied away from the red and black marble urged upon him. Such marble might be fine indeed, the client agreed, but to speed up the construction he chose instead the conventional New York brownstone.

The three Vanderbilt houses, the last of which vanished in 1946, did impress one Edward Strahan, who wrote the text for a most luxurious album on this addition to the Avenue. "We are permitted," said Strahan, "to make a revelation of a private home which . . . may stand as a representative of the new impulse now felt in the national life. Like a more perfect Pompeii, the work will be the vision and image of a typical American residence, seized at the moment when the nation begins to have a taste of its own. . . . The country at this moment" —he was writing in 1881—"is just beginning to be astonishing."

The curious thing was that neither William Henry nor his wife sought to be astonishing. Mrs. Vanderbilt was extremely reluctant to leave her old home farther down the Avenue; this was evident in Strahan's description of her bedroom: "In this exquisite room, where silver toilet services, embroidered silks and delicate hangings vie with masterly paintings to refresh the attention, it would seem that dreams must be propitious and the waking pleasant. Among the fragile glitter of the upholstery, where everything seems to start bright and crisp from the hands of the artificer, there is one worn-looking object, and only one: it is the little Bible."

It was only in contemplating the afterlife that the second generation of the family was magnificent. William Henry showed real judgment when it came to the Vanderbilt Mausoleum erected in 1885 atop a knoll at New Dorp on Staten Island. The view of the harbor was noble. So was the landscaping by Olmsted. Most impressive was the vast tomb itself. This was the work of Richard Morris Hunt, the first American to graduate from the Ecole des Beaux-Arts.

Hunt's first sketch for the mausoleum failed to please. "You entirely misunderstand me; this will not do at all," Vanderbilt corrected his architect. "We are plain, quiet, unostentatious people, and we don't want to be buried in anything as showy as that would be. The cost of it is a secondary matter and does not concern me. I want it roomy and solid and rich. I don't object to appropriate carvings, or even statuary, but it mustn't have any unnecessary fancy-work in it." Whereupon Hunt solved the problem by referring to the Romanesque precedent of the chapel of Saint-Gilles at Arles.

He had faced many a problem in Paris—"If other countries teach you as France has taught you, you will do great things!" was the comment of his master Hector Lefuel, with whom he planned the pavilion on the Place du Palais Royal of the New Louvre—but he met no challenge abroad to compare with that offered by the former Alva Smith of Mobile, Alabama, the determined woman who married the Commodore's grandson William Kissam Vanderbilt in the spring of 1875. "She's a wonder," Hunt admitted. "It's as much as one man's brain can do to keep up with the Vanderbilt work."

It was plain that Alva Vanderbilt was not the type of patron he had in mind when he told one of his staff that "the first thing you've got to remember is that it's your clients' money you're spending. Your business is to get the best result you can, following their wishes. If they want you to build a house upside down, standing on its chimney, it's up to you to do it and still get the best possible result."

It was also clear that Mrs. Vanderbilt believed the time had come to alter the appearance of Manhattan Island. She might even have agreed with the

Richard Morris Hunt

Stanford White

Alva Vanderbilt

*At the time this picture was taken, she had divorced W. K. Vanderbilt to become
Mrs. O. H. P. Belmont. Women's Suffrage was the cause closest to her heart in
her last years.*

complaint of her old acquaintance Edith Wharton. "How could I understand," Mrs. Wharton wrote in her autobiography, "that people who had seen Rome and Seville, Paris and London, could come back to live contentedly between Washington Square and the Central Park? What I could not guess was that this little low-studded rectangular New York, cursed with its universal chocolate-covered coating of the most hideous stone ever quarried, this cramped horizontal gridiron of a town without towers, porticoes, fountains or perspectives, hide-bound in its deadly uniformity of mean ugliness, would fifty years later be as much a vanished city as Atlantis or the lowest layer of Schliemann's Troy."

Alva Vanderbilt played a certain role in bringing about the change that Edith Wharton noticed. When she came to consider the proper mansion for her family, she turned to Hunt, and Hunt responded. He had run into the Duc d'Aumale—to use the final title of the prince of the House of Orléans whose detestation of the tricolor made it impossible for him to assume the throne as Henri V—often enough in Paris, and he could not have missed visiting the Duc's new château at Chantilly, begun in 1876 by Daumet in the manner of the early French Renaissance. Could the new Chantilly have set him thinking about something similar over here? In any event, Hunt was inspired by Blois and possibly by the mansion of Jacques Coeur at Bourges when the Vanderbilt commission came into his office. But the W. K. Vanderbilt château, completed in 1881 on the northwest corner of Fifth Avenue and Fifty-second Street, was no replica. It was a superb evocation of the Renaissance in Caen stone. The problem of the correct house for a millionaire had been solved.

Shortly to be solved as well was the question of the Vanderbilts' rank in New York society. The Commodore, as his best friend would have told you, was given to profanity, and Mrs. William Backhouse Astor, the acknowledged queen of the Four Hundred, had hesitated for many years to call on the Vanderbilts. She reckoned without Alva. On the twenty-sixth of March, 1883, Mrs. W. K. Vanderbilt staged in her new and noble home the most brilliant ball in the history of Manhattan Island. One of the most impatient of all the guests was Mrs. Astor's daughter Carrie, who had been practicing day after day the steps of the Star Quadrille for the great event. She had become letter-perfect when Alva let it be known that since Mrs. Astor had never called, Miss Carrie could not very well be invited. Stunned by this ultimatum, Mrs. Astor dispatched a footman with her card: the Vanderbilts had at last arrived. For certain people the Vanderbilt ball was almost as important as the opening fifty-eight days later of John and Washington Augustus Roebling's Brooklyn Bridge.

Alva Vanderbilt's triumph was to have great consequences, as her daughter Consuelo, soon to be driven to marry the ninth Duke of Marlborough, suspected. "I still remember," Consuelo set down in her autobiography, "how long and terrifying was that dark and endless upward sweep as, with acute sensations of fear, I climbed to my room every night, leaving below the light and its comforting rays. For in that penumbra there were spirits lurking to destroy me, hands stretched out to touch me and sighs that breathed against my cheek. . . . I prayed for courage to reach the safety of my room."

One of the consequences was that Richard Morris Hunt never again knew an idle moment. Turning back again and again to the French Renaissance, not only in Newport but New York, he conceived the palace of Mrs. Astor and her son John Jacob on the northeast corner of Fifth Avenue and Sixty-fifth Street and that of Elbridge T. Gerry on the southeast corner of Sixty-first Street, besides assisting his pupil George Browne Post in the design of Cornelius Vanderbilt II's château on the west side of the Avenue between Fifty-sixth and Fifty-seventh Streets. Like the W. K. Vanderbilt mansion, these have all been destroyed, but nothing could destroy Hunt's impact: New York was to become a Renaissance city.

Another consequence was that Jacob Riis, a Danish immigrant who explored the slums with desperate devotion, redoubled his efforts for decent housing for the poor. It was not an accident that his *How the Other Half Lives: Studies Among the*

Tenements of New York was published in the same year that Mrs. Astor's friend Ward McAllister gave us *Society as I Have Found It.* "I have read your book and I have come to help" was the message that Police Commissioner Theodore Roosevelt left at Riis's office. One of those who helped the most was the philanthropist Alfred T. White, whose Brooklyn tenements are still worth a visit in the twentieth century. "In those days," White has written, "no one liked to be known as a tenement-house owner because there were no tenements fit to own. There was then a very general misconception that poor people preferred such surroundings as they had and did not desire either sunshine or fresh air. . . . All these misconceptions were happily corrected." Although Professor William Graham Sumner told his students at Yale in the year of the Vanderbilt ball that "God and nature have ordained the chances and conditions of life on earth once for all," there were those who disagreed.

Still another consequence was that the newly founded firm of McKim, Mead & White, who had gone far indeed in the direction of modern architecture, reversed themselves to become the foremost advocates of a return to the Renaissance. Partner Charles Follen McKim, we are told by his biographer, made a practice of strolling up Fifth Avenue late at night for a good long look at the Vanderbilt château. Having taken a look at it, he could enjoy another cigar before turning in. He always slept better for the sight of it.

Like his associate Stanford White, McKim had been trained in the office of Henry Hobson Richardson, the genius who came out of the Ecole des Beaux-Arts to create Trinity Church, Boston, in 1872. Occasionally carelessly described as Romanesque, Trinity was more than a derivative monument. Its simple, magnificent massing enchanted a generation. Its designer settled in New York in 1865 on his return from Paris, but by 1874 he had moved to Brookline, Massachusetts, possibly because he sensed that Manhattan craved splendor—the very domain that modern architects, with the marvelous exception of Louis Sullivan in the Chicago Auditorium, have so far failed to invade.

Richardson built but little in New York State. He made the experiment of designing himself a mansardic cottage at Arrochar on Staten Island, planned the State Hospital at Buffalo and collaborated on the capitol, but the only commission that exhibited his gifts was the Albany City Hall.

How much McKim, Mead & White learned from him may be guessed by glancing at the (now destroyed) town house of the craftsman Louis C. Tiffany, and at two singular achievements in the shingle style: the house and stables of Cyrus Hall McCormick at Richfield Springs, and the estate at Mamaroneck of Charles J. Osborn.

Osborn was the confidential broker of Jay Gould, but did not figure as large in the life of Manhattan as Henry Villard, the German-born railway promoter who walked into the McKim, Mead & White office with a proposal for five adjoining houses on the east side of Madison Avenue between Fiftieth and Fifty-first Streets. According to one legend, the draftsman Joseph M. Wells was the man who suggested that here was the chance to outdo Hunt by following Renaissance precedents. This is possible, but there is no question that the design of the Villard complex was the work of White himself. Calling on Maitland Armstrong to contribute the mosaic work in Villard's own front hall, and on Augustus Saint-Gaudens to sculpt the clock on the Villard stairs, White succeeded in creating the most distinguished town house or houses ever built on Manhattan Island.

It may even have been too distinguished. In 1885, when Villard moved in, the Northen Pacific he headed was in difficulty, and threatening crowds gathered in the street, imagining that he was to occupy all five of the houses he had planned for himself and four friends. The crowds were unaware of the fact, reported by his son Oswald Garrison Villard, that he made the move to save money on hotel bills.

Like Hunt, White was no plagiarist in his best work. Although the Villard complex was supposed to be a "copy" of the Cancelleria in Rome, a palace once attributed to Bramante, the only significant resemblance between the two buildings is the detailing about the windows. The plans are totally dissimilar, the model being a trapezoid enclosing a cortile, while the alleged replica is U-shaped. The important thing was that White proved he could invent just as elegant but a far more livable setting than Hunt.

Like no other residence, that of Villard offered the perfect stage for the pageantry New Yorkers came to demand of the very rich. If you happen to believe that pageantry is inexcusable, you may decide that White betrayed the cause of modern architecture. In a sense this accusation is true, for few did more to prepare the way for Frank Lloyd Wright than McKim, Mead & White in their early work. But you will have to concede that the firm caught, as did no other, the spirit of Manhattan. The merchandising and financial capital of America demanded splendor: what, then, was more appropriate than this return to the Renaissance?

It was not a matter of chance that McKim, Mead & White planned fifty-seven clubhouses. Of these the most successful was McKim's University Club, subtly evoking the Palazzo Strozzi in Florence, but there is no reason to neglect White's work at the Century and at the Metropolitan Club. This last was said to have been founded by J. P. Morgan when out of sorts with the old Union Club; to mention Morgan is to recall the Pierpont Morgan Library, over which McKim struggled so patiently that the banker complained that it was not his library but McKim's.

But Morgan was only one of the superb New Yorkers who could conceive of no other architects to contrive the scenery for their best performances. White himself was often on hand to watch his clients on stage. "He was pervasive," wrote his good friend the critic John Jay Chapman. "Not a day passed without hearing something new about him. His flaming red head could be seen a mile; and every night at the Opera he would come in late, not purposely advertising himself, but intuitively knowing that every millionaire in town would see him, and that the galleries would whisper, and the very supers on the stage would mutter: *There's Stanford White.*

"He swam," Chapman continued, "on a wave of prestige that lifted him into view like a Triton that typified the epoch. If you were walking down Fifth Avenue and caught sight of a Turkey-red curtain at the upper window of a new Renaissance apartment, you knew who it was who had hung his flag there. If you went to a charity ball and saw on the stage a set of gilt twisted wooden columns eighteen feet high and festooned with laurel, you looked around until you found Stanford on top of a ladder draping a tapestry."

It was no wonder that White was asked to create Louis Sherry's ballroom, the Tiffany store on Fifth Avenue and the Herald Building for the irrepressible publisher James Gordon Bennett, Jr. White was inescapable in the New York of the 1890s. Nor did he cater uniquely to the rich and the well-born. His Madison Square Garden was for every New Yorker in search of pleasure. Close at hand was his Madison Square Presbyterian Church, where the Reverend Charles H. Parkhurst Sunday after Sunday damned Tammany Hall from the pulpit.

Since the glorious commission for Pennsylvania Station fell to McKim, you might suppose that the partners never knew a second of anxiety. This was not the case. When White exceeded the budget for the Fifth Avenue mansion of Payne Whitney, Colonel Oliver H. Payne of Standard Oil, who was paying the bills for his nephew's new house, did not conceal his displeasure.

"I know," White apologized, *"that all kinds of small extras have crept in and that the changes I made in the smaller rooms have added over a hundred thousand dollars to the price of the house, and I have dreaded to speak to you about it until the house was far enough finished for you to see the result, as although I feared that you would be angry at first, I thought if you saw the money had been wisely spent and that I had given Payne and Helen a house to live in which was really of the first water and could stand in beauty with any house in the world, that you would forgive me and I believed in my heart that you would in the end approve of what I had done, but your saying to me yesterday that you could not see where the money has gone has taken all the sand out of me and made me very unhappy, for I know from the*

character of the work and in comparison with other houses that it is not extravagant." It was fortunate that White had an ally in Mrs. Whitney, the daughter of John Hay. "I am dreadfully sorry about the fits the Colonel gave you and can't quite see what it was all about," she wrote.

Charles Follen McKim could never be discouraged. In 1909, the year of his death, he did his best to raise the hopes of White's son in Paris, then completing his studies at the Ecole. "Uncle Sam," said McKim, "is now proud of what is being done, and is going to demand the very best that millions can purchase; and there is no fear of falling back into the degenerate order of things which has hitherto always existed. Mr. Hunt was the pioneer and ice-breaker who paved the way for recognition of the profession by the public; and now his successors are paving the way for 'vous autres,' who are to come home and design the *really great works.* . . . When you get through with your work on the other side and come home ready to build, you will find opportunities awaiting you that no other country has offered in modern times. The scale is Roman, and it will have to be sustained."

This may be the proper moment to risk a reassessment of the eclectics whose work was once dismissed because based on historical precedent. We know nowadays, when only modern buildings are erected, that modern architecture may be good, bad or indifferent. The very same thing may be said of the eclectics' achievements. Although McKim, Mead & White are open to criticism for the dullness of the Columbia campus, the partners usually succeeded in maintaining the highest standards, despite the volume of business that engulfed the office.

Nor did McKim, Mead & White lack intelligent disciples. One of these was Charles Adams Platt, who had no formal training for the profession, but made an acute study of Italian architecture and gardens while preparing to be an etcher in Paris. He was too wise to perpetrate a replica, but his thorough knowledge of Vignola and the other Italian masters was evident in the country house at Barrytown he designed in 1914 for White's friend John Jay Chapman.

Far more important, so far as Manhattan Island was concerned, was the firm of Warren & Wetmore, who laid out both Grand Central Station and the adjoining New York Central Building. Although the engineers Reed & Stem may deserve the credit for the station's marvelous ramps and the shrewd elevated roadways speeding traffic up and down Park Avenue, the architects were responsible for the noble ornamentation of these two buildings. As an example of city planning, they stand—or stood—unrivaled, providing a perfect focus for mid-Manhattan.

Neither Warren nor Wetmore seem to have questioned their approach to the demands of the twentieth century, but Thomas Hastings, the partner of John Merven Carrère, was a man given to doubts. "Copying," he admitted, "destroys progress in art. The problem solved makes style." And looking back at his own work on the Fifth Avenue elevation of the New York Public Library, which does reveal a careful study of the Perrault façade for the Louvre, he argued that "our Renaissance must not be merely archaeological. To build a French Louis XII or Francis I or Louis XIV house, or to make an Italian *cinquecento* design, is indisputably not modern architecture."

Ernest Flagg, who like Carrère and Hastings was a most loyal graduate of the Ecole, translated doubt into action in the fanciful glass façade of the Singer Building at 561 Broadway, proving in 1902 that he was much more imaginative in exploiting the uses of transparency than most of the purveyors of the curtain wall sixty years later.

The contribution of the eclectics to American architecture may one day seem greater than uncompromising modernists supposed. But it is obvious in 1969 that New York City has not yet played the role in modern architecture that its resources promised. There is only one building by Sullivan in Manhattan, the much abused Bayard Building on Bleecker Street, and only one example of Wright, the Guggenheim Museum.

There were skyscrapers in late-nineteenth-century Manhattan, but it is doubtful that Richard Morris Hunt's Tribune Building or George Browne Post's Western Union Building will ever be compared with the work of Burnham & Root in Chicago or with the masterpieces of Louis Sullivan in St. Louis or Buffalo. Perhaps there was something in the air that discouraged architects from rejoicing in the solution of the practical problems of the skeleton frame.

When the brilliant art dealer Samuel Bing visited the United States in 1893 on a mission for the French government, he was overwhelmed by what he saw of the work of Richardson and Sullivan and summed up in *La Culture Artistique en Amérique* what he believed to be their credo. "The art of architecture," wrote Bing, "owes its vitality to a complete comprehension of the practical laws to which it is subservient." This was not the same thing as saying that the art of architecture could be mastered by arriving at a perfect estimate of the cost per square foot. What fascinated Bing was the exhilaration that is sure to come to a great artist who has successfully met the most matter-of-fact demands of a client.

This exhilaration was evident in Ernest Flagg's Singer Tower of 1908 at 149 Broadway. Though destroyed in 1968, the masterful façade of this eclectic skyscraper will never cease haunting the imagination of those who believe that a great building is the record of a personality. With Louis Sullivan, Flagg might have exclaimed that "ornament . . . should appear, when completed, as though . . . there by the same right that a flower appears amid the leaves of its parent plant."

Raymond Hood, who won the international competition for Chicago's Tribune Tower in 1922 by recalling with his associate John Mead Howells the Tour de Beurre at Rouen, was as impersonal in his approach to the skyscraper as Flagg was personal. He might also be judged a follower of Adolf Loos of Vienna, who published a curious essay in 1908 entitled *Ornament and Crime*. "Tattooed men who are not under arrest are either latent criminals or degenerate aristocrats," Loos argued at the height of his campaign against decoration in any form. He should have been pleased by Hood's Daily News Building and McGraw-Hill Building of 1930, which were stripped of all—or nearly all—ornament. Hood was also moving in the direction of architecture by committee, for it is difficult to decide what was his exact contribution to the development of Rockefeller Center, the last of whose original units was completed in 1940. Nevertheless, Rockefeller Center marked a certain progress. For the first time since the Grand Central Station of 1913, there was real provision for vast crowds. Unhappily, the plazas that Hood and his many associates introduced have never been imitated, and the owners of the Seagram Building found they were penalized under the city tax laws for permitting an open space before their tower.

Architecture by committee has never again been so considerate of the public. Nor has it produced a monument as welcome as Rockefeller Center. A typical example is the United Nations Headquarters, which represents the collaboration of Wallace K. Harrison; Voorhees, Walker, Foley & Smith; and Skidmore, Owings & Merrill, with the advice of a design board that included Le Corbusier, Niemeyer from Brazil and Nowicki from Poland.

This undistinguished landmark may be said to have set the precedent for the Pan Am Building by Emory Roth & Sons with the collaboration of Walter Gropius and Pietro Belluschi, but it must be admitted that Harrison and his partners did no damage to surrounding cityscape. The Pan Am Building is no less than a studied insult to Grand Central Station and the New York Central Building: the huge concrete box that towers above the station has succeeded in obliterating the focus provided by Warren & Wetmore, besides adding to the intolerable congestion of this area of Manhattan. "Architecture is teamwork," Gropius has often observed. It is apparent that he had no intention of co-operating with architects who were dead and distinguished. Most recently Gropius' old associate and admirer Marcel Breuer has proposed that another box be placed atop Grand Central itself.

So much for the wanton destruction of a great achievement in city planning. The monumentality of Grand Central seems to have made no impression on Wallace K. Harrison and Max Abramowitz when they planned the new Opera House and Philharmonic Hall for Lincoln Center, nor did they make any provision for traffic to compare with the efforts of Reed & Stem more than fifty years before.

The characteristic of New York City architecture since the Second World War is of course the curtain wall, or glass façade, which is assumed to be the answer to every problem posed by the skyscraper, just as the brownstone front a hundred years earlier was the solution to the real-estate speculator's private house. No history of the curtain wall could omit Flagg's first Singer Building at 561 Broadway, nor should you neglect the Hallidie Building of 1918 in San Francisco by Willis J. Polk. But in its unadorned form the curtain wall may be traced most easily to the unexecuted projects of Ludwig Miës van der Rohe in Berlin as early as 1919. Here was the formula and, in its scrupulous if impersonal elegance, the ancestor of the Seagram Building which he and Philip Johnson erected at 375 Park Avenue in 1955.

The Seagram Building is the curtain wall at its best. There is, however, a vast difference between the sophistication of Miës and the bland performance of the firm of Skidmore, Owings & Merrill, who completed Lever House in 1952 and the Manufacturers' Hanover Trust Company Building in 1954. Whether the Park Avenue of the 1960s, which owes so much to SOM and to their imitators, is an improvement over that of the 1920s, as planned by Warren & Wetmore and McKim, Mead & White, is open to question. The curtain wall can be a bore.

Architects who presume to be individuals have done little building in postwar New York, and Frank Lloyd Wright's Guggenheim Museum is a constant threat to the peace of mind of art critics who believe that a museum should be as impersonal as a cash register after business hours. There has been, however, one notable exception in the suburbs. Paul M. Rudolph's Endo Pharmaceutical Plant at Garden City, completed in 1966, is an eloquent demonstration of what may be accomplished by a designer who will not lower the banner of imagination. Changing from second to second as the sunlight plays upon its undulating forms, the Endo Plant is an excellent example of what Le Corbusier had in mind when he described architecture as "le jeu savant, correct et magnifique des volumes assemblés sous la lumière."

And in New York City Eero Saarinen had the courage to disregard the vogue for the curtain wall when he received the commission for the CBS Building on the northeast corner of Sixth Avenue and Fifty-second Street. Its massive black granite piers proclaim that a mind and not a computer was in charge of the drafting-room. "Our architecture," the frequently dissatisfied Saarinen announced, "is too humble. It should be prouder, much richer and larger than we see it today." He did his part, not only at CBS but in inventing the incomparable sculptured forms of the TWA Terminal at Kennedy. The tradition of his office, which insisted on judging every job as a challenge to be solved without relying on precedents, has been maintained after his death in 1961 by his successors, Roche & Dinkeloo Associates, who produced the Ford Foundation Building on East Forty-second Street in 1967.

As for the future of architecture on Manhattan Island and in the state, it depends first of all on the architects, who must choose between being the accomplices of real-estate promoters and being their own free agents. It also depends upon the clients. Manhattan may not need another return to the Renaissance, but it does need a client or two with the spunk of Alva Vanderbilt. "I always do everything first," she said. "I was the first of my set to marry a Vanderbilt." She could scarcely approve of the new Metropolitan Opera House, whose concrete façade has the nobility of cardboard. But she would be certain to appreciate an architect who dared.

"I do not know what is untried and afterward," wrote Walt Whitman. "But I know it is sure, alive, sufficient." He could have been speaking for the greatest architect who will ever appear in New York.

Res. Christopher Billopp, Hylan Boulevard and Satterlee Street, Tottenville, Staten Island, c. 1700 (architect unknown). This is also known as the Conference House. Here on September 11, 1776, Lord Howe conferred with Benjamin Franklin, John Adams and Edward Rutledge on possible terms of peace. Open to the public.

Res. Jean Hasbrouck, New Paltz, c. 1712 (architect unknown). The village was founded by French Protestant refugees in 1677 and named after the Rhenish Pfalz, where they settled before moving to the New World. Open to the public.

Res. Jan Van Dusen, Hurley, c. 1744 (architect unknown). The New York Committee of Safety is known to have met in this house during the American Revolution.

Res. Frederick Van Cortlandt, Van Cortlandt Park, Bronx, 1748 (architect unknown). This comfortable, unpretentious dwelling was the best the aristocracy of New York could afford in the middle of the eighteenth century. The manor of Cortlandt had been granted to Stephen Van Cortlandt in 1697. Open to the public.

Exterior and interior of Philipse Manor Hall, northwest corner of Warburton Avenue and Dock Street, Yonkers, c. 1719–1745 (architect unknown). The First Lord of Philipseborough Manor and the builder of this house was Frederick Philipse, once the official carpenter of the Dutch West India Company. It was in this house that Mary Philipse, sister of the Third Lord, was married to Major Roger Morris in 1758. From 1868 to 1908 the Manor House served as the Yonkers City Hall. Open to the public by the New York State Historic Trust.

Res. General Philip Schuyler, southwest corner of Clinton and Schuyler Streets, Albany, 1762 (architect unknown). Here in 1780 Schuyler's daughter was married to Alexander Hamilton. Open to the public by the New York State Historic Trust.

Johnson Hall, res. Sir William Johnson, Johnstown, 1763 (architect unknown).
Open to the public by the New York State Historic Trust.

OPPOSITE ABOVE: *Fort Johnson, res. Sir William Johnson, Fort Johnson, 1749 (architect unknown). This, the third Mohawk Valley home of the man who did so much to rally the Indians to the British cause in two French wars, is now open to the public as the Museum of the Montgomery County Historical Society.* OPPOSITE BELOW: *Guy Park, res. Colonel Guy Johnson, West Main at Henrietta Street, Amsterdam, 1773 (architect unknown). Built for Sir William Johnson's daughter and her husband (his nephew), Guy Park is open to the public by the New York State Historic Trust. The house was reconstructed in 1848, and the flanking two-story wings date from 1858.*

Saint Paul's Chapel, Broadway between Fulton and Vesey Streets, New York City, 1766 (Thomas McBean, architect. The steeple was added by James C. Lawrence in 1793–94). George Washington worshipped in this, the oldest surviving church building on Manhattan Island.

8

Interior, Saint Paul's Chapel. The altar-screen is the work of Pierre-Charles L'Enfant, 1787.

Res. Roger Morris, West 160th Street at Jumel Terrace, New York City, 1765 (architect unknown). Morris, who served with Washington on Braddock's staff, married Mary Philipse of Philipse Manor. Later the house belonged to Madame Stephen Jumel, the very good friend of Aaron Burr. It is doubtful indeed that the two-story portico dates back to 1765; more than likely it was added at a later period, as was the arched entrance door. Open to the public.

F E D E R A L   H A L L

The Seat of Congress

Federal Hall, northeast corner of Wall and Nassau Streets, New York City, 1789 (Pierre-Charles L'Enfant). L'Enfant remodeled the old City Hall to serve as the temporary national capitol from 1789 to 1790, when the government was moved to Philadelphia. Demolished. This is the engraving by Amos Doolittle of the drawing of Peter Lacour.

Res. Gurdon Conkling, Rensselaerville, 1825 (Ephraim Russ).

Res. Daniel Conkling, Rensselaerville, 1806 (Ephraim Russ).

Res. Eli Hutchinson, Rensselaerville, 1823 (Ephraim Russ). Settled by Connecticut families at the end of the eighteenth century, Rensselaerville lies about twenty-five miles southwest of Albany.

13

ABOVE: *Res. Gideon Granger, 295 North Main Street, Canandaigua, 1814 (architect unknown). There is a certain temptation to assume that Joseph-Jacques Ramée was the architect of this house for the Postmaster General under Jefferson and Madison, for the front elevation is not unlike that of Øregaard, a villa Ramée designed in Copenhagen in 1806, but there is no documentary evidence to support such an attribution.* BELOW: *Belvedere, res. Philip Church, Angelica, 1808 (Edward Probyn). Angelica, slightly west of Hornell in Allegany County, was settled by French refugees in the early nineteenth century. One settler of Anglo-Saxon stock was Philip Church, son of the John Barker Church—alias John Carter—who was Alexander Hamilton's brother-in-law.*

Lorenzo, res. John Lincklaen, Cazenovia, 1807 (architect unknown). Lincklaen, the Amsterdam-born local agent for the Holland Land Company, named the town after Théophile Cazenove, general agent for the enterprise. Lincklaen's mansion is now open to the public by the New York State Historic Trust.

Res. Jacques LeRay de Chaumont, Leraysville, 1806–08 (architect unknown). LeRay, who was Madame de Staël's landlord at the castle of Chaumont, was one of the French investors in the present counties of Jefferson and Lewis. The house is now on the grounds of Camp Drum military reservation.

The Hill, res. Henry W. Livingston, south of Hudson, c. 1796 (architect unknown). The Hill was the first house of the Livingston family to show any architectural distinction, although the Livingstons were nothing if not distinguished at the beginning of the nineteenth century. Henry had served in Paris as the secretary of our minister, Gouverneur Morris.

More prominent than Henry W. Livingston were Robert R. Livingston, Chancellor of New York and Jefferson's minister to France during the Louisiana negotiations, and his brother Edward Livingston, Mayor of New York and Secretary of State and minister to France in the Jackson Administration. Among those who married into the family were General Richard Montgomery, Governor Morgan Lewis, Robert Fulton and John Armstrong, minister to France under Jefferson. The founder of the family was Robert Livingston, a Scot who married Alida Schuyler, the widow of Nicholas Van Rensselaer in 1679, five years after he landed in Albany. By 1686 his landholdings (ultimately consisting of 160,000 acres in Dutchess and Columbia Counties) were erected into a manor.

*New York City Hall, Broadway at City Hall Park, New York City, 1803–12
(Joseph-François Mangin and John McComb, Jr.).*

New-York Historical Society

LEFT: *Saint John's Chapel, east side of Varick Street between Beach and Laight Streets, New York City, 1803–07 (John McComb, Jr., and Isaac McComb). Demolished.* BELOW: *Saint John's Park or Hudson Square. Demolished. The town houses built around the chapel marked a greater advance in city planning than Washington Square. Fenimore Cooper, who was charmed by the park, made it the site of the opening of his novel* Home as Found. *Here he led his Americans just back from Europe to sample the conversational gifts of New Yorkers.*

New-York Historical Society

South Hall, Union College, Schenectady, 1813 (Joseph-Jacques Ramée).

LEFT: *Chapel, Hamilton College, Clinton, 1828 (Philip Hooker).*
BELOW: *Albany Academy, Lafayette Park, Albany, 1815 (Philip Hooker). Renamed after the scientist Joseph Henry, the Academy houses the Albany Department of Education.*

Hyde Hall, res. George Hyde Clark, Cooperstown, 1811–13 (Philip Hooker). The interiors were restored after the First World War by Lawrence Grant White, son of Stanford White. Open to the public by the New York State Historic Trust.

ABOVE: *Holland Land Office, West Main Street, Batavia, 1815 (architect unknown). It is possible that Joseph Ellicott, surveyor for the gigantic land speculation in which Robert Morris joined, was the architect of this remarkable little building with its portico of four Roman Doric columns. Open to the public as a museum.* BELOW: *Old Union Hotel, Sackets Harbor, 1817 (architect unknown).*

ABOVE: *Stone Barn, Shaker Settlement, New Lebanon, 1827?* *(architect unknown)*. BELOW: *Trustees' Building, Shaker Settlement, New Lebanon, 1827?* *(architect unknown)*. *"Buildings, mouldings and cornices, which are* merely for fancy, *may not be made by believers,"* wrote the Shaker Father Joseph Meacham in his Millennial Laws.

Two views of Lyndhurst, res. William Paulding, Tarrytown, 1838–65. Enlarged in 1865 for the second owner, George Merritt, Lyndhurst was piously preserved by Jay Gould and his daughters. It is open today to the public by the National Trust for Historic Preservation.

Lyndhurst from the bank of the Hudson. "I have never seen anything to equal it," Andrew Jackson Downing reported to Davis.

25

ABOVE: *Entrance to Lynd-hurst.* BELOW: *Dining-room of Lyndhurst.* "*If you see anything offensive to your gothick eye (you don't squint, so no offense), put your veto upon it,*" wrote William Paulding's son to Davis when the interiors were being completed.

Res. Henry Delamater, Rhinebeck, 1844. Delamater was a Rhinebeck banker.

Res. E. B. Strange, Dobbs Ferry, 1855. This is preserved as Saint Christopher's School for Boys. Strange was a silk importer.

Res. John J. Herrick, Tarrytown, 1855. The castle of this merchant has been demolished, after serving the purposes of Miss Mason's School.

Res. C. B. Sedgwick, Syracuse, 1845. The Gothic cottage of this attorney has been demolished.

ABOVE: *New York University, Washington Square, New York City, 1833–35. Ithiel Town collaborated with Davis on this commission. Demolished. Richard Morris Hunt appears to have been amused by this Gothic campus. At least, he posed for the character of Henry Stillfleet in Theodore Winthrop's novel of 1860, Cecil Dreeme. When asked if the college were defunct, Stillfleet-Hunt replies: "Not defunct, only without vitality. The trustees fancied that, if they built roomy, their college would be populous; if they built marble, it would be permanent; if they built Gothic, it would be scholastic and mediaeval in its influences; if they had narrow, mullioned windows, not too much disorganising modern thought would penetrate."* BELOW: *House of Mansions, southeast corner of Fifth Avenue and Forty-second Street, New York City, 1858. Demolished. This housing development was sponsored by the carpet manufacturer Alvan Higgins.*

SUBURBAN GOTHIC VILLA.

Phelps-Stokes Collection, New York Public Library

Res. William H. C. Waddell, northwest corner of Fifth Avenue and Thirty-seventh Street, New York City, 1844, as drawn by Davis. Demolished. Mrs. Waddell, famous in her day for the bals poudrés *she gave in this villa, spent her old age in a hotel room, her husband having lost his fortune in the panic of 1857. She may not have been amused by* Fashion and Famine, *a dime novel published by Ann Sophia Stephens in 1855, which used the villa for its setting.*

31

*Res. John Cox Stevens, southeast corner of Murray Street and College Place,
New York City, 1845, as drawn by Davis. Demolished.*

Unidentified interior drawn by Davis.

Original clubhouse of the New York Yacht Club, Hoboken, N.J., 1846. When this photograph was taken, the clubhouse had been moved to Glen Cove, Long Island. Today it stands at Mystic, Conn.

ABOVE: *Res. John Munn, Utica, 1855. This banker's town house is an example of what Davis could accomplish in the "Italian villa" style so popular in the 1850s.* BELOW: *Montgomery Place, res. Mrs. Edward Livingston, Barrytown, 1843–63. The original house was completed in 1805 by Janet Livingston Montgomery, widow of the general who died in the capture of Montreal in 1775. On the sixth of July, 1818, his ashes, destined to be finally entombed in the east front of Saint Paul's Chapel in New York City, were borne down the Hudson by steamboat. Mrs. Montgomery no sooner glanced at the steamer from her veranda than she fell to the floor in a swoon. Davis' opportunity came in 1843, when Mrs. Edward Livingston, widow of Jackson's minister to France, asked him to remodel the house completely. Thinking of the superb furniture the Livingstons had brought back from Paris, he composed a façade that would have seemed most elegant in 1801, when Edward Livingston was made Mayor of New York. In 1863 he made further alterations for the family.*

Res. E. C. Litchfield, Prospect Park, Brooklyn, 1854. Now Prospect Park Head-quarters, this Italian villa was designed for the railroad promoter who was treas-urer of the first line tying Chicago to the eastern seaboard.

Offices of the nursery firm of Ellwanger & Barry, Rochester, 1854.

OPPOSITE: *Trinity Church, Broadway at Wall Street, New York City, 1839–46. As Phoebe Stanton has pointed out in her* Gothic Revival and American Church Architecture, *Trinity owes much to an "ideal church" published in A. W. Pugin's* True Principles. *The one mistake that Upjohn made was in not giving Thomas Cole the chance to paint a picture or design a window for Trinity. "We are too much fettered by puritanical opinion to allow us to place an altarpiece, even," Cole wrote Gulian C. Verplanck in the spring of 1844.*

Church of the Ascension, northwest corner of Fifth Avenue and Tenth Street, New York City, 1841. By buying up for himself the land immediately to the rear, Dr. Manton Eastburn, the Low Church rector of Ascension, foiled the architect's desire to provide a deep chancel. In 1888 the altar was redesigned by Stanford White, Augustus Saint-Gaudens and Maitland Armstrong, complete with a mural by John La-Farge.

Church of the Holy Communion, northwest corner of Sixth Avenue and Twentieth Street, New York City, 1845.

Res. C. T. Longstreet, Syracuse, 1851. Demolished. This castle, which later housed the School of Journalism of Syracuse University, was built for the first clothier to ship ready-made suits to California in the gold rush.

Main Building, Vassar College Poughkeepsie, 1865. This was one of the great American tributes to the mansard roofs of the Second Empire.

OPPOSITE ABOVE: *Grace Church, northeast corner of Broadway and Tenth Street, New York City, 1846.* OPPOSITE BELOW: *Rectory, Grace Church, New York City, 1847. Like many men of high moral principles, the diarist George Templeton Strong knew his own mind when it came to art and architecture. Renwick, he decided, was an "infatuated monkey. . . . Nature cut him out for a boss carpenter and the vanity and pretension that are endurable and excusable in an artist are not to be endured in a mechanic." Fortunately, there were few who agreed with Strong.*

41

Rockefeller Center

Saint Patrick's Cathedral, Fifth Avenue between Fiftieth and Fifty-first Streets, New York City, 1858–79.

ABOVE: *Beverwyck, res. William Paterson Van Rensselaer, Washington Avenue at Eighth Street, Rensselaer, 1840–43 (Frederick Diaper). Now Saint Anthony's School, this Italian villa was the home of one of Thomas Cole's first important patrons. For him Cole painted* The Departure *and* The Return, *today in the collection of the Corcoran Gallery. Diaper was best known for his commercial buildings in Manhattan.* BELOW: *Res. Washington Irving, Tarrytown, 1836 (George Harvey). Open to the public by the Sunnyside Restoration.*

Astor House, northwest corner of Broadway and Vesey Street, New York City, 1836 (Isaiah Rogers). Demolished.

Old Library, U.S. Military Academy, West Point, 1841 (Isaiah Rogers). Although Rogers was responsible for this Gothic library and for the Egyptian entrance to the Jewish cemetery at Newport, he specialized in Greek Revival hotels. Aside from the Astor House, he planned the Tremont House in Boston and the Maxwell House in Nashville.

Presbyterian or Whaler's Church, Madison Street between Main and Union Streets, Sag Harbor, 1844 (Minard Lafever). The tower has been missing since the hurricane of 1938.

Res. Benjamin Hunting, Main and Garden Streets, Sag Harbor, 1845 (Minard Lafever). Now the Suffolk County Whaling Museum of Sag Harbor.

Exterior and interior, Church of the Holy Trinity, northeast corner of Clinton and Montague Streets, Brooklyn, 1847 (Minard Lafever).

46

Fonthill, res. Edwin Forrest, West 261st Street at Palisade Avenue, Bronx, 1848 (architect unknown). Now the library of the College of Mount Saint Vincent, Fonthill was built for the indomitable Shakespearean actor Forrest, who was forced to sell his home after spending $200,000 divorcing his wife in the proper histrionic style.

Res. Seabury Tredwell, 29 East Fourth Street, New York City, 1832 (architect unknown). Open to the public as "The Old Merchant's House."

ABOVE: *Gate Lodge, res. Gardiner Howland, New Hamburgh, c. 1841 (architect unknown). Philip Hone was pleased by this seat just south of Poughkeepsie. "It is a princely residence, the abode of elegant hospitality, and all the comforts that heart and body can desire," he declared in his diary. The house is demolished.*
BELOW: *Lafayette Terrace, 428–434 Lafayette Street, New York City, 1832–33 (architect unknown). These four adjoining houses were once attributed to A. J. Davis.*

ABOVE: *Res. J. B. Chollar, Watervliet, c. 1848 (architect unknown). Demolished. Jay Gould featured this Gothic villa on his Albany County map.* BELOW: *Smith-Blythe house, Ashville, c. 1835 (architect unknown). One of the smarter advertisements of the Greek Revival in Chautauqua County.*

Res. Timothy Brown, Georgetown, c. 1850 (Timothy Brown). Brown was famous in Madison County as a spiritualist, but could never convince his wife of the wisdom of his faith.

OPPOSITE ABOVE: *Res. Francis Cottenet, Dobbs Ferry, 1852 (Detlef Lienau).* OPPOSITE BELOW: *Res. Carl Carmer, Irvington-on-Hudson, 1860–70 (architect unknown). Begun in 1860 by a certain Philip Armour, it was at first a typical example of the octagonal style advocated by Orson Squire Fowler; late in the 1860s it was acquired by Joseph Stiner, an importer of Chinese teas and spices, who replaced the original mansard roof by the present dome. In 1947 the house passed into the hands of Carl Carmer, author of* Dark Trees to the Wind, The Hudson *and* Listen for a Lonesome Drum, *who is well aware that he owns one of the prizes of New York State in the romantic era.*

North side of Washington Square, New York City, c. 1830 (architect unknown).
This view of the square was taken before many of the recent mutilations.

Res. Henry Ten Eyck, Cazenovia, 1847 (architect unknown). This Gothic villa, which could have been inspired by one of Downing's books, serves as the town hall in 1969.

53

ABOVE: *Res. Agnes Calhoun Sheldon, Randolph, 1850–55 (architect unknown).*
Randolph is in the neighborhood of Jamestown. BELOW: *The Mansion, Oneida*
Community, Oneida, 1860 (architect unknown). This was the community house
of the Perfectionists, who settled here under the guidance of John Humphrey
Noyes. Once the center of a utopian communist community, Oneida is today the
headquarters of the firm producing silver-plated tableware.

Rose Hill, res. A. Boody, Geneva, c. 1835 (architect unknown).

Res. John Schoolcraft, Jr., Guilderland, c. 1840 (architect unknown). The uncle of the explorer Henry Rowe Schoolcraft, John Schoolcraft, Jr., once managed a hotel in Hamilton, as Guilderland was formerly named.

OPPOSITE ABOVE: *Gate Lodge, res. John Reade Stuyvesant, Hyde Park, 1840 (architect unknown). Stuyvesant's house has vanished; in 1969 the estate belongs to the Jesuit school of Saint Andrew's on Hudson.* OPPOSITE BELOW: *Res. Cornelius Ormes, Panama, 1833 (John Capple). Capple is only one of the many Chautauqua County architects and carpenters rediscovered by Jewel Helen Conover in her* Nineteenth Century Houses in Western New York.

Res. Amoniah Atherly, Ashville, c. 1835 (architect unknown).

"House of Seven Gables," Busti, 1850? (architect unknown).

Copp house, Sinclairsville, c. 1853 (architect unknown).

Res. Sardius Seward, Panama, c. 1840 (John Capple).
Pages 58 and 59 begin to illustrate the variety of Chautauqua County.

59

ABOVE: *A. T. Stewart Building (later Wanamaker's), southeast corner of Broadway and Tenth Street, New York City, 1862 (James Kellum). Demolished.* BELOW: *Haughwout Building, northeast corner of Broadway and Broome Streets, New York City, 1857 (J. P. Gaynor). The cast-iron glory of the old A. T. Stewart store was destroyed by fire after the premises were abandoned. The Haughwout Building is an equally important monument of the cast-iron age: it boasted the first practical passenger elevator, the invention of Elisha Graves Otis.*

ABOVE: *Laing Stores, northwest corner of Washington and Murray Streets, New York City, 1848 (James Bogardus).* BELOW: *Eccentric Mills, corner of Center and Duane Streets, New York City, 1848 (James Bogardus). Demolished.*

Museum of the City of New York

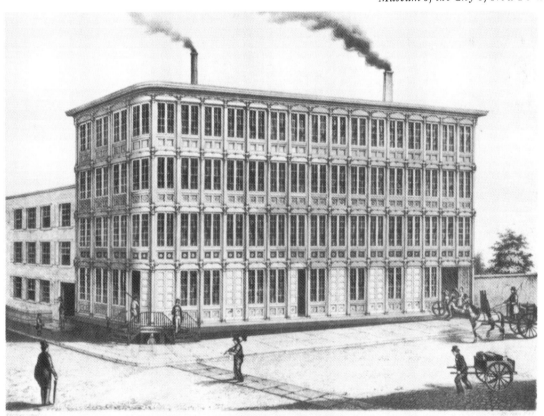

REPRESENTATION OF
THE FIRST CAST IRON HOUSE ERECTED.
Invented by JAMES BOGARDUS, Builder of CAST IRON HOUSES and Manufacturer of
THE ECCENTRIC MILL, &c. corner of CENTRE & DUANE STREETS.

Brown Brothers

Brown Brothers

Grand Union Hotel, Broadway between Washington and Congress Streets, Saratoga Springs, 1872 (architect unknown). Demolished. Commodore Vanderbilt was only one of the many millionaires who enjoyed their cigars on this veranda.

OPPOSITE ABOVE: *Res. Leonard W. Jerome, southeast corner of Madison Avenue and East Twenty-sixth Street, New York City, 1866 (Thomas R. Jackson). Demolished.* OPPOSITE BELOW: *Res. A. T. Stewart, northwest corner of Fifth Avenue and Thirty-fourth Street, New York City, 1869 (John Kellum). Demolished. Of these two mansardic town houses, the more elegant—quite naturally—was that of the onetime Vanderbilt broker Jerome, whose daughter Jennie was the mother of Sir Winston Churchill. The Jerome mansion was later the Manhattan Club.*

ABOVE: *Res. Webster Wagner, Palatine Bridge, 1877 (Horatio Nelson White). Wagner was the designer of the sleeping cars of the New York Central before the Vanderbilts took notice of those of George Mortimer Pullman.* BELOW: *Harmony Cotton Mills, Cohoes, 1866 (architect unknown). No one has done more to make Americans appreciate the charms of their late-nineteenth-century commercial architecture than the painter Edward Hopper, who seems to have had his influence on the photographer of this scene.*

Syracuse Savings Bank, 120 North Salina Street, Syracuse, 1876 (Joseph Lyman Silsbee). The designer of this Ruskinian bank later moved to Chicago, where he gave Frank Lloyd Wright his first job. "I adored Silsbee," said Wright in his autobiography. "He had style."

ABOVE: *Mercantile Library, Montague Street between Clinton and Court Streets, Brooklyn, 1869 (Peter Bonnett Wight). Demolished.* BELOW: *National Academy of Design, northwest corner of Twenty-third Street and Fourth Avenue, New York City, 1863 (Peter Bonnet Wight). Demolished. The Ruskinian Wight also moved to Chicago, where he trained in his office both Daniel Hudson Burnham and John Wellborn Root.*

Museum of the City of New York

66

Mechanics and Farmers' Bank, Albany, 1874–75 (Russell Sturgis). This Ruskinian could never forgive McKim, Mead & White for their advocacy of the Renaissance.

ABOVE: *Belfry, Olana, res. Frederic E. Church, near Hudson, 1874 (Frederic E. Church and Calvert Vaux). Olana is open to the public by the New York State Historic Trust.* BELOW: *Landscaping of Olana, attributed to Frederick Law Olmsted.*

Two views of Olana.

69

The Great Hall of Olana and the Front Parlor.

70

Rooftop of Olana.

71

Res. William H. Vanderbilt and his daughters Mrs. Elliott F. Shepard and Mrs. William D. Sloane, Fifth Avenue between Fifty-first and Fifty-second Streets, New York City, 1881 (John B. Snook and Herter Brothers). Demolished. W. H. Vanderbilt occupied 640 Fifth Avenue on the left; Mrs. Sloane, 642 Fifth Avenue; Mrs. Shepard, 2 West Fifty-second Street. The last to be destroyed was 640 Fifth Avenue, the last occupant of which was Mrs. Cornelius Vanderbilt III.

Library of W. H. Vanderbilt, as decorated by Herter Brothers.

THE ADVENT OF
RICHARD MORRIS HUNT

ABOVE: *Saint Mark's Church, Islip, Long Island, 1880 (Richard Morris Hunt).* BELOW: *The Studio Building, 51 West Tenth Street, New York City, 1856 (Richard Morris Hunt). Demolished. In neither Saint Mark's nor the Studio Building could Hunt reveal his ambition: Alva Vanderbilt had not yet appeared on the horizon. But the Studio Building was the retreat of many well-known artists, including William Merritt Chase. It was in Chase's studio that John Singer Sargent arranged for Carmencita to dance for Isabella Stewart Gardner.*

The Vanderbilt Mausoleum, Moravian Cemetery, New Dorp, Staten Island, 1885 (Richard Morris Hunt).

Music Room, res. W. K. Vanderbilt, 660 Fifth Avenue, New York City, 1881 (Richard Morris Hunt). Demolished.

Res. W. K. Vanderbilt, 660 Fifth Avenue, New York City, 1881 (Richard Morris Hunt). Immediately to the right may be seen 666 Fifth Avenue, the residence of W. K. Vanderbilt, Jr., by Stanford White. Both mansions demolished.

Living room, res. Cornelius Vanderbilt II, west side of Fifth Avenue between Fifty-seventh and Fifty-eighth Streets, New York City, 1882–94 (George B. Post). Hunt came to the aid of his former pupil in completing the tower on the Fifth Avenue side. Others who collaborated with Post were the painter John LaFarge and the sculptors Karl Bitter and Augustus Saint-Gaudens.

Byron Collection, Museum of the City of New York

Res. Cornelius Vanderbilt II, 1882–94 (George B. Post). Demolished.

Res. Elbridge T. Gerry, southeast corner of Fifth Avenue and Sixty-first Street, New York City, 1891 (Richard Morris Hunt). Demolished. Gerry, in whose veins flowed the blood of the Goelets, was a passionate patron of the Society for the Prevention of Cruelty to Children. His passion was occasionally misplaced, as when the Society, in the spring of 1894, banned the performance of a fifteen-year-old girl in Gerhart Hauptmann's Hannele's Assumption.

Exterior, res. Mrs. William B. Astor and Mr. & Mrs. John Jacob Astor IV, northeast corner of Fifth Avenue and Sixty-fifth Street, New York City, 1891 (Richard Morris Hunt). Demolished.

81

Living room, res. Mrs. William B. Astor (Richard Morris Hunt).

Brooklyn Bridge, Brooklyn, 1867–83 (John August and Washington Augustus Roebling). John August Roebling lost his life working on the bridge in 1869, when a ferry boat crushed his leg. His son was afflicted with caisson disease before the bridge was completed; on May 24, 1883, when the bridge was dedicated, he had to watch the ceremony, crippled, half-paralyzed and blind, from the window of his home on Columbia Heights.

OPPOSITE ABOVE: *Alfred T. White's Riverside Houses, 4–30 Columbia Place, Brooklyn, 1890 (William Field & Son).* OPPOSITE BELOW: *Alfred T. White's Tower & Home Apartments, Hicks Street between Warren and Baltic Streets, Brooklyn, 1878–79 (William Field & Son). The Riverside Houses were sliced in half for the Brooklyn-Queens Expressway.*

THE IMPORTANCE OF
HENRY HOBSON RICHARDSON

State Hospital, 400 Forest Avenue, Buffalo, 1871 (H. H. Richardson).

Albany City Hall, Eagle Street between Maiden Lane and Pine Street, Albany, 1880–81 (H. H. Richardson).

Res. H. H. Richardson, Arrochar, Staten Island, 1868–69 (H. H. Richardson).
Richardson's first thought, on his return from Paris, was not to show off all he
had learned at the Ecole, but to prove his skill in the local mansardic vernacular.

Saint Mary's Church, Tuxedo Park, 1885 (William Appleton Potter).

Gate Lodge to Tuxedo Park, Tuxedo Park, 1885 (Bruce Price). William Appleton Potter, brother of Bishop Henry Codman Potter, and Bruce Price were two architects immediately influenced by Richardson's example. Tuxedo Park, on the edge of the Ramapo Mountains, was a real-estate development sponsored by Pierre Lorillard IV.

86

Cathedral of Saint John the Divine, New York City, 1892 (project by W. Halsey Wood). The Episcopal Diocese of New York could have built this masterpiece in the Richardsonian manner by W. Halsey Wood. Instead it endorsed the efforts of Heins & LaFarge, Cram & Ferguson, Adams & Woodbridge and the other architects who have never succeeded in completing the Cathedral.

De Vinne Press Building, northeast corner of Lafayette and East Fourth Streets, New York City, 1885–86 (Babb, Cook & Willard). Like Potter and Price, Babb, Cook & Willard owed much to Richardson in their early work.

OPPOSITE ABOVE: *Res. Cyrus Hall McCormick, Richfield Springs, 1882.* OPPOSITE BELOW: *Stables, res. Cyrus Hall McCormick, Richfield Springs, 1882. It was White himself who supervised the extraordinary decoration of the stables. The house is now demolished.*

ABOVE: *Gate Lodge, res. C. J. Osborn, Mamaroneck, 1885.* BELOW: *Res. C. J. Osborn, Mamaroneck, 1885. White was also the partner in charge of this commission. Recently the house has been used as a country club.*

David G. Farragut Memorial, northeast corner of Madison Square, New York City, 1880–81. The statue of the admiral who won the battle of Mobile Bay in 1864 is the work of Augustus Saint-Gaudens, but the pedestal, foretelling the triumphs of the Art Nouveau in Europe in the next decade, is mainly the achievement of Stanford White.

Byron Collection, Museum of the City of New York

Res. Louis Comfort Tiffany, southeast corner of Madison Avenue and Seventy-second Street, New York City, 1885. Demolished. Here the great designer maintained a studio on the top floor. The house was commissioned by his father, Charles L. Tiffany, founder of the famous silver and jewelry store. McKim, Mead & White also created the Tiffany & Company store on the southeast corner of Fifth Avenue and Thirty-seventh Street (see page 101).

North end of the Villard mansions, Madison Avenue between Fiftieth and Fifty-first Streets, New York City, 1885. In 1969 the Archdiocese of New York occupies most of the Villard complex.

Clock on the stairs of the Villard mansion, 1885 (Stanford White with Augustus Saint-Gaudens).

Museum of the City of New York

Res. W. K. Vanderbilt, Jr., 666 Fifth Avenue, New York City, 1905. Demolished. This may be the most tactful building ever erected on Manhattan Island; White could not have paid a more graceful compliment to Hunt's château next door for W. K. Vanderbilt, Sr.

OPPOSITE ABOVE: *Herald Building, Herald Square, New York City, 1893. Demolished. The Palazzo del Consiglio in Verona may have prompted White's imagination in this instance.* OPPOSITE BELOW: *Louis Sherry ballroom, 522 Fifth Avenue, New York City, 1898. Demolished. For the great caterer, White planned not only this ballroom but also a small hotel above.*

ABOVE: *Metropolitan Club, northeast corner of Fifth Avenue and Sixtieth Street, New York City, 1894.* BELOW: *Century Club, 7 West Forty-third Street, New York City, 1891.*

University Club, northwest corner of Fifth Avenue and Fifty-fourth Street, New York City, 1899.

Pierpont Morgan Library, 33 East Thirty-sixth Street, New York City, 1906.
The Palazzo del Te at Mantua may have been the inspiration for this façade.

East Room, the Pierpont Morgan Library. It was in the Library, on the second of November, 1907, that Morgan put an end to the panic that followed the failure of the Knickerbocker Trust Company.

Madison Square Presbyterian Church, Madison Square, New York City, 1906.
Demolished.

Tiffany Building, southeast corner of Fifth Avenue and Thirty-seventh Street, New York City, 1906. This building has been mutilated to meet the supposed needs of the Horn & Hardart restaurant chain. It once was an evocation of the Palazzo Cornaro in Venice.

Exterior, Pennsylvania Station, Seventh Avenue between Thirty-first and Thirty-third Streets, New York City, 1906–10.

Inner concourse, Pennsylvania Station.

Outer concourse, Pennsylvania Station. The station, which once was dismissed as a "replica" of the Baths of Caracalla, had come to mean much to modern architects by the time it was destroyed in 1963. The parade protesting the demolition was led by Philip C. Johnson and the widow of Eero Saarinen.

Res. Joseph Pulitzer, 11 East Seventy-third Street, New York City, 1903. The mansion of the publisher of the New York World *has been divided into apartments.*

OPPOSITE ABOVE: *Dining room, res. Payne Whitney, 972 Fifth Avenue, New York City, 1903.* OPPOSITE BELOW: *Exterior, res. Payne Whitney. Whitney's father was the William Collins Whitney whose ballroom is reproduced on page 107. The Payne Whitney mansion is now occupied by the Cultural Services of the French Embassy.*

Museum of the City of New York

105

Museum of the City of New York

Museum of the City of New York

Museum of the City of New York

Ballroom, res. William Collins Whitney, 871 Fifth Avenue, New York City, 1900. Demolished. White did not build this mansion for the master-millionaire of the traction ring, but only redecorated it. Whitney was a client worth cultivating. As Henry Adams observed, "he had thrown away the usual objects of political ambition like the ashes of smoked cigarettes, satiated every taste, gorged every appetite, won every object that New York afforded, and, not yet satisfied, had carried his field of activity abroad, until New York no longer knew what most to envy, his horses or his houses."

OPPOSITE ABOVE: *Exterior, res. Clarence H. Mackay, Roslyn, Long Island, 1902.* OPPOSITE BELOW: *Dining room, res. Clarence H. Mackay. Now demolished, Harbor Hill, the Mackay estate, was the site in 1924 of the great ball for the Prince of Wales. Eight hundred were invited; twelve hundred were made welcome.*

Mrs. Mackay, who demanded a somewhat literal translation of the château of Maisons near Paris, was one of White's more difficult clients. However, there were compensations. There were wine-racks for 21,900 bottles in this mansion's cellar, and White descended on antique dealers in Munich, Dresden, Berlin and Vienna; Florence, Palermo and Malta; Barcelona, Burgos, Seville, Cordova and Madrid; Oporto and Lisbon; Brussels, Amsterdam and London; Bordeaux, Marseilles and Paris in his endless quest for ideal chairs and irreproachable tapestries.

"Although it may be a calamity to you, you must acknowledge that, in the end, you will get a pretty fine château on the hill, and with the exception of Biltmore, I do not think there will be an estate equal to it in the country," White wrote Mackay to calm his fears. There were times when this client, whose father had struck it rich in the Comstock Lode, was frightened. "In regard to the remaining mooseheads which you strongly advise me to buy, and of which I understand you made a hurried inspection, you seem to forget the main point, viz: the price," he once notified White. In the end he spent $840,000 on the house.

107

Res. James L. Breese, Southampton, Long Island, 1906. Now an economics study center for Amherst College, this country house is an excellent example of the freedom with which White played with the Colonial Revival.

OPPOSITE ABOVE: *Ruins of the res. E. D. Morgan, Wheatley Hills, Long Island, 1891.* OPPOSITE BELOW: *Casino for John Jacob Astor IV, Rhinecliff, 1898.*
  McKim was the partner in charge of the country home of the grandson of New York's Civil War Governor; White was in charge at Rhinecliff.

Detail, Madison Square Garden, Madison Square, New York City, 1890. Demolished.

On the block bounded by Madison Avenue, Fourth Avenue and Twenty-sixth and Twenty-seventh Streets, White planned not only a home for the annual horse show, but a theater, restaurant, concert hall and roof garden. Of yellow brick and Pompeian white terra cotta, the Garden was one of the great civic monuments of Manhattan, and no one could complain that the architect had remembered the Giralda at Seville while sketching the tower. Here White was murdered by the rowdy millionaire Harry Thaw in 1906.

Tower, Madison Square Garden.

111

Dakota Apartments, northwest corner of Central Park West and Seventy-second Street, New York City, 1882–84. The architect was only thirty-five when he began this splendid apartment house in a somewhat German Renaissance manner.

Plaza Hotel, Central Park South and Fifth Avenue, New York City, 1906–07. This French Renaissance hotel was a favorite not only with Frank Lloyd Wright, who always stayed here when in town, but also with Le Corbusier, who took a particular pleasure in telling priggish students of modern architecture that he was most fond of "vast and beautiful hotels that are not at all modern, *but have acquired a past thanks to their rich upholstery."*

DANIEL HUDSON BURNHAM

Flatiron (or Fuller) Building, Broadway at East Twenty-third Street and Fifth Avenue, New York City, 1901–03. Co-designer in his early years with John Wellborn Root of many important Chicago skyscrapers in the Richardsonian manner, Burnham later swore by the Renaissance tradition upheld by Hunt and McKim, Mead & White. Here is Burnham in his later, classical manner.

Brown Brothers

Produce Exchange, Bowling Green on Beaver Street, New York City, 1884. Demolished. As Nathan Silver has pointed out, the Produce Exchange boasted a true iron skeleton, and was completed a year before William Le Baron Jenney's Home Insurance Building in Chicago, generally considered to be the first skyscraper—i.e., first tall building with skeleton frame. Post may have been an eclectic, but he was an eclectic who cannot be ignored by serious students of modern architecture.

*Res. James Stillman, 9 East Seventy-second Street, New York City, 1894–96.
Number 7, the town house on the left, was designed in 1899 by Flagg & Chambers. H. T. Sloane was the first owner of the Stillman house. In his old age Stillman, for many years the president of the National City Bank of New York, moved to Paris, where he collected the paintings of Mary Cassatt and went with her to watch, fascinated, the showings of the great couturiers. Apparently he did know how to enjoy himself, although he proclaimed in his last years: "I have never in all my life done anything I wanted and cannot now."*

116

New York Public Library, Fifth Avenue and Forty-second Street, New York City, 1902–09. The figures above the fountains are the work of Frederick Mac-Monnies, c. 1920, and the lions the work of Edward Clark Potter, 1911. The model for the Fifth Avenue façade of the library is the east front of the Louvre planned by Claude Perrault in 1668 with the assistance of Louis LeVau and Charles LeBrun.

Detail, portico, res. Henry Clay Frick.

Two views, res. Henry Clay Frick (now the Frick Collection), Fifth Avenue between Seventieth and Seventy-first Streets, New York City, 1913–14. Frick, the most vigilant of all the lieutenants of Andrew Carnegie in the steel business, earned the first millions with which this eighteenth-century French palace was built from the coal and coke lands of western Pennsylvania.

119

Grand Central Station, East Forty-second Street between Vanderbilt and Lexington Avenues, New York City, 1903–13. The engineers on the job were Reed & Stem and Colonel William J. Wilgus. Above the station may be seen part of the Pan Am Building, 1963, the work of Emery Roth & Sons with Pietro Belluschi and Walter Gropius. It is interesting that Walter Gropius, who headed the school of architecture at Harvard after founding the Bauhaus in his native Germany, always hesitated to expose his students to architectural history. "When the innocent beginner is introduced to the great achievements of the past, he may be too easily discouraged from trying to create for himself," he warned.

Detail, Grand Central Station.

The Grand Central main hall in the days before it was rented out for advertising space.

Grand Central as it looked before Walter Gropius.

New York Central Building, 230 Park Avenue, Forty-fifth to Forty-sixth Streets,
New York City, 1929.

The New York Yacht Club, 37 West Forty-fourth Street, New York City, 1899.

Res. James A. Burden, 7 East Ninety-first Street, New York City, 1902. Mrs. Burden was the great-granddaughter of Commodore Cornelius Vanderbilt. Her sister, Mrs. John Henry Hammond, lived next door at 9 East Ninety-first Street, in the mansion designed by Carrère & Hastings in the same year. The Burden house is now the Duchesne Residence School.

124

Res. Otto H. Kahn, 1 East Ninety-first Street, New York City, 1918. Kahn was the banker who was the patron of the poet Hart Crane. His mansion, designed by Gilbert with J. Armstrong Stenhouse, is now the Convent of the Sacred Heart.

Tower of the Singer Building, 149 Broadway, New York City, 1906–08. Demolished.

*Singer Building, 149 Broadway, New York City,
1897–98. The tower was an addition. Demolished.*

Singer Building, 561 Broadway, New York City, 1902–04.

Res. Frederick G. Bourne (now the LaSalle Military Academy), Oakdale, Long Island, c. 1902. Bourne was an executive of the Singer Company.

Scribner Building, 597 Fifth Avenue, New York City, 1913. The Scribner Building houses not only the Scribner Book Store but also the offices of the publishing firm.

St. Regis-Sheraton

Entrance, St. Regis Hotel, 2 East Fifty-fifth Street, New York City, 1902–04. With the Plaza, the St. Regis, launched by John Jacob Astor IV, is the last survivor of the elegant hotels built before the First World War.

Two views, res. John Jay Chapman, Barrytown, c. 1914. The brilliant essayist John Jay Chapman was one of Stanford White's deepest admirers.

ABOVE: *Res. Willard Straight (now the Audubon Society), northeast corner of Fifth Avenue and Ninety-fourth Street, New York City, 1913–15. First a diplomat in the Far East and later a banker, Straight married the daughter of William Collins Whitney and founded* The New Republic. BE-LOW: *Union Club, 101 East Sixty-ninth Street, New York City, 1932. William Adams Delano and his partner, Chester H. Aldrich, won their first big commission, the Walters Gallery in Baltimore, thanks to their presence on board the yacht of Cornelius Vanderbilt III in Venice. Close at hand was moored the yacht of Henry Walters.*

Res. William A. M. Burden, Syosset, Long Island, 1916. Mrs. Burden, later Mrs. Richard Tobin, was a great-granddaughter of Commodore Cornelius Vanderbilt.

Res. at 7 East Ninety-sixth Street, New York City, 1915. Codman, a Bostonian who lived and died in France, where he became an authority on châteaux, was the collaborator of Edith Wharton on her first book, The Decoration of Houses *(1897). "Privacy," Mrs. Wharton pointed out with Codman at her elbow, "would seem to be one of the first requisites of civilized life, yet it is only necessary to observe the planning and arrangement of the average house to see how little this need is recognized. Each room in a house has its individual uses: some are made to sleep in, others are for dressing, eating, study or conversation; but whatever the uses of a room, they are seriously interfered with if it be not preserved as a small world by itself."*

134

Wildenstein Gallery, 19 East Sixty-fourth Street, New York City, 1931. "He never did a drawing after he set up the office," remarked one of the assistants of Horace Trumbauer after his death. The draftsman responsible for this exquisite Louis XV building—as for the now vanished Duveen Gallery—may have been the Negro Julien Abele, who probably also designed the James B. Duke and James Speyer mansions. Frank Seeberger, an earlier employee of Trumbauer, may have executed the mansion of George Jay Gould.

Wildenstein & Co.

ABOVE: *Res. James Speyer, 1058 Fifth Avenue, New York City, 1914. Demolished. The Speyers, the wealthiest Jewish family of Frankfurt in the eighteenth century, later moved their banking firm to London and New York.* BELOW: *Res. James B. Duke, 1 East Seventy-eighth Street, New York City, 1909. Now the Fine Arts Center of New York University, this mansion of the tobacco millionaire was modeled after the Hôtel Labottière in Bordeaux by Laclotte.*

Brown Brothers

Res. George Jay Gould, 1 East Sixty-seventh Street, New York City, 1908. Demolished. The son of Jay Gould, George Jay Gould was once the boss of the Missouri Pacific, Denver & Rio Grande and Wabash railroads, but his brothers and sisters were dissatisfied with his management of the estate, and the lawyers' fees for the litigation absorbed $2,703,635. The mansion was later occupied by Mrs. Cornelius Vanderbilt II (after the demolition of her château) and by her daughter the Countess Lâszló Széchényi.

Detail, cottage at Kamp Kill Kare. Best remembered for his monumental National Gallery in Washington, D.C., Pope could be informal and almost Californian in spirit, as in this estate in the Adirondacks for Francis P. Garvan, Alien Property Custodian in the First World War.

OPPOSITE ABOVE: *Entrance, Kamp Kill Kare, Raquette Lake, c. 1918.* OPPOSITE BE-LOW: *Lakeside cottages at Kamp Kill Kare.*

Woolworth Building, Broadway between Park Place and Barclay Street, New York City, 1911–13. This Gothic-clad skyscraper was designed by the architect not only of the United States Customs House on Bowling Green but also of the Capitol of Minnesota and the Detroit Public Library.

Saint Bartholomew's Church, Park Avenue between Fiftieth and Fifty-first Streets, New York City, 1917–23. In the days when Goodhue's former partner Ralph Adams Cram was reckoned an outstanding architect, Goodhue himself was considered "modern" in the design of the Capitol of Nebraska. The portico on this Byzantine church was designed by McKim, Mead & White c. 1902–03 for the previous Saint Bartholomew's on Madison Avenue.

Fireplace, Veterans' Room, Seventh Regiment Armory, Park Avenue between Sixty-sixth and Sixty-seventh Streets, New York City, 1880. The gifted designer of glass was in partnership at this time with Samuel Colman and Candace Wheeler.

Laurelton Hall, res. Louis Comfort Tiffany, Oyster Bay, Long Island, 1904. Demolished. Completely designed by Tiffany without the assistance of a professional architect, Laurelton Hall became a retreat for artists subsidized by the Louis Comfort Tiffany Foundation.

Decorative panel from the Guaranty Building, now the Prudential Building, southwest corner of Church and Pearl Streets, Buffalo, 1894–95. Sullivan was still in partnership with Dankmar Adler when he designed this, the greatest sky-scraper in New York State.

The Guaranty Building.

*Cornice from the Bayard Build-
ing, now the Condict Building,
65–69 Bleecker Street, New
York City, 1897–98. At this
time Sullivan was associated
with Lyndon P. Smith.*

Lower stories of the Bayard Building.

Res. Darwin D. Martin, Buffalo, 1904. This mansion for the chief executive of the Larkin Company has now been restored to serve as the residence of the president of the State University of New York at Buffalo.

*Exterior, Larkin Company Administration Building, 680 Seneca Street, Buffalo,
1904. Demolished. Elbert Hubbard was once the sales manager of this soap-
manufacturing concern.*

Interior, Larkin Company Administration Building.

Res. E. E. Boynton, Rochester, 1908.

Res. Walter V. Davidson, Buffalo, 1908.

Two views, res. W. R. Heath, Buffalo, 1905. Heath was the brother-in-law of Elbert Hubbard.

Res. Sol Friedman, Pleasantville, 1949.

Another view, res. Sol Friedman.

Exterior, the Guggenheim Museum.

OPPOSITE: *Interior and exterior, Solomon R. Guggenheim Museum, Fifth Avenue between Eighty-eighth and Eighty-ninth Streets, New York City, 1959.*

McGraw-Hill Building, 330 West Forty-second Street, New York City, 1930.
The partnership of Hood, Godley & Fouilhoux produced this building.

New York Daily News Building, 220 East Forty-second Street, New York City, 1930.

Rockefeller Center, Fifth to Sixth Avenues, West Forty-eighth to Fiftieth Streets, New York City, 1931–1940. Rockefeller Center represents the collaboration of Reinhart & Hofmeister, Corbett, Harrison & MacMurray, and Hood & Fouilhoux.

Ezra Stoller Associates: Esto

Seagram Building, 375 Park Avenue, New York City, 1955. Miës's partner on this building was Philip C. Johnson.

Manufacturers Hanover Trust Company, 510 Fifth Avenue, New York City, 1954.

Lever House, 390 Park Avenue, New York City, 1952.

WALLACE K. HARRISON

United Nations Headquarters, United Nations Plaza, First Avenue between Forty-second and Forty-eighth Streets, New York City, 1947–53. Harrison headed the committee of architects on this enterprise.

Two views, Kneses Tiffereth Israel Synagogue, 575 King Street, Port Chester, 1956.

164 *Exterior and interior, Munson-Williams-Proctor Institute Museum, 310 Genesee Street, Utica, 1960.*

Res. Gilbert Tompkins, Hewlett, Long Island, 1946.

Whitney Museum, southeast corner of Madison Avenue and Seventy-fifth Street, New York City, 1966. Hamilton Smith was Breuer's partner on this commission. The museum was founded by the sculptress Gertrude Vanderbilt Whitney, wife of Harry Payne Whitney, daughter-in-law of William Collins Whitney, and great-granddaughter of Commodore Cornelius Vanderbilt.

166

OPPOSITE: *Two views, First Unitarian Church, 220 Winton Street South, Rochester, 1964.*

167

Kleinhans Music Hall, Symphony Circle, Buffalo, 1938. Eero Saarinen worked with his father on this commission. In charge of construction were the Buffalo architects F. J. and W. A. Kidd.

OPPOSITE: *Two views, Motel on the Mountain, Hillburn, 1956. Associated with the great California architect Harwell Hamilton Harris on this commission was the firm of Perkins & Will.*

Metropolitan Opera House, Columbus Avenue between Sixty-third and Sixty-fourth Streets, New York City, 1966 (Wallace K. Harrison).

OPPOSITE ABOVE: *New York State Theater, Columbus Avenue between Sixty-second and Sixty-third Streets, New York City, 1964 (Philip C. Johnson and Richard Foster).* OPPOSITE BELOW: *Philharmonic Hall, Columbus Avenue between Sixty-fourth and Sixty-fifth Streets, New York City, 1962 (Max Abramowitz).*

Another view of the Endo Pharmaceutical Plant.

OPPOSITE: *Endo Pharmaceutical Plant, Stewart Avenue at Endo Boulevard, Garden City, Long Island, 1966.*

Ford Foundation Building, 320 East Forty-third Street, New York City, 1967.

174

Two views, International Business Machines Research Center, Yorktown Heights, 1961. The statue is the work of Seymour Lipton.

CBS Photo

CBS Building, 51 West Fifty-second Street, New York City, 1965.

OPPOSITE: *Two views, Noyes Hall, Vassar College, Poughkeepsie, 1958.*

Two views of the exterior, TWA Terminal, Kennedy Airport, Queens, 1962.

Interior, TWA Terminal.

BIBLIOGRAPHY

Before beginning a formal listing, I should like to salute the author or authors of the exasperatingly comprehensive essay on architecture in *New York: A Guide to the Empire State* (Oxford University Press, 1940). The hints about unusual buildings in this WPA guide have been worrying me for over twenty-five years, provoking the excursions on which this book is based.

Albion, Robert G., *The Rise of New York Port, 1815–1860*, New York, 1939.

Andrews, Edward D., *The People Called Shakers*, New York, 1953.

Andrews, Wayne, "Alexander Jackson Davis," *Architectural Review*, May, 1951.

——, "America's Gothic Hour," *Town & Country*, November, 1947.

——, *Architecture, Ambition and Americans*, New York, 1955.

——, *Architecture in America*, New York, 1960.

——, "McKim, Mead & White: Their Mark Remains," *The New York Times*, January 7, 1951.

——, *Mr. Morgan and His Architect*, New York, 1957.

——, "New York's Own Architects," *New-York Historical Society Quarterly*, January, 1951.

——, *The Vanderbilt Legend*, New York, 1941.

Bailey, Rosalie F., *Pre-Revolutionary Dutch Houses and Families in Northern New Jersey and Southern New York*, New York, 1936.

Baldwin, Charles C., *Stanford White*, New York, 1931.

Balsan, Consuelo Vanderbilt, *The Glitter and the Gold*, New York, 1952.

Bing, Samuel, *La Culture Artistique en Amérique*, Paris, 1896.

Bogardus, James, *Cast-Iron Buildings: Their Construction and Advantages*, New York, 1856.

Brown, Roscoe C. E., *Church of the Holy Trinity*, New York, 1922.

Burnham, Alan, "Forgotten Engineering," *Architectural Record*, April, 1959, and May, 1960.

——, "The New York Architecture of Richard Morris Hunt," *Journal of the Society of Architectural Historians*, May, 1952.

——, ed., *New York Landmarks*, Middletown, 1963.

Carmer, Carl, *Dark Trees to the Wind*, New York, 1949.

——, *The Hudson*, New York, 1939.

——, *Listen for a Lonesome Drum*, New York, 1936.

Chapman, John Jay, "McKim, Mead & White," *Vanity Fair*, September, 1919.

Condit, Carl W., *American Building Art: 20th Century*, New York, 1961.

Conover, Jewel Helen, *Nineteenth Century Houses in Western New York*, Albany, 1966.

Cooper, James Fenimore, *Home as Found*, New York, 1860.

——, *Notions of the Americans*, 2 v., Philadelphia, 1836.

Le Corbusier, *Quand les Cathédrales étaient blanches*, Paris, 1937.

Cortissoz, Royal, *Monograph of the Work of Charles A. Platt*, New York, 1913.

Creese, Walter, "Fowler and the Domestic Octagon," *Art Bulletin*, June, 1946.

Delafield, John R., "Montgomery Place," *Yearbook*, Dutchess County Historical Society, 1929.

Downing, Andrew J., *The Architecture of Country Houses*, New York, 1958.

——, *Cottage Residences*, New York, 1846.

——, *Rural Essays*, New York, 1853.

——, *A Treatise on the Theory and Practice of Landscape Gardening*, New York, 1860.

Eberlein, Harold D., "Hurley Town: A New Netherland Suburb," *American Suburbs*, May, 1911.

The First Hundred Years, Otis Elevator Co., New York, 1953.

Foerster, Bernd, *Architecture Worth Saving in Rensselaer County*, New York, Troy, 1965.

Fox, Dixon Ryan, *Yankees and Yorkers*, New York, 1940.

Fowler, Orson S., *A Home for All*, New York, 1854.

Gray, David, *Thomas Hastings, Architect*, Boston, 1933.

Hall, Edward H., *Philipse Manor Hall, Yonkers, New York*, New York, 1912.

Hamlin, Talbot F., *Greek Revival Architecture in America*, New York, 1944.

Hislop, Codman, and Harold A. Larrabee, "Joseph-Jacques Ramée and the Building of North and South Colleges," *Union College Alumni Monthly*, February, 1938.

Hitchcock, Henry Russell, *The Architecture of H. H. Richardson and His Times*, New York, 1936.

Huntington, David C., *The Landscapes of Frederic Edwin Church: Vision of an American Era*, New York, 1966.

Huxtable, Ada Louise, *Classic New York*, New York, 1964.

Keller, William, "Rensselaerville, an Old Village of the Helderbergs," *White Pine Series of Architectural Monographs*, Vol. 10, No. 4, 1924.

Kimball, Fiske, *Domestic Architecture of the American Colonies and of the Early Republic*, New York, 1922.

Kimball, LeRoy E., "The Old University Building and the Society's Years on Washington Square," *New-York Historical Society Quarterly*, July, 1948.

Koch, Robert, *Louis C. Tiffany, Artist in Glass*, New York, 1964.

Kouwenhoven, John A., *The Columbia Historical Portrait of New York*, New York, 1953.

Kramer, E. W., "Detlef Lienau, Architect of the Brown Decades," *Journal of the Society of Architectural Historians*, March, 1955.

Lafever, Minard, *The Architectural Instructor*, New York, 1856.

——, *The Beauties of Modern Architecture*, New York, 1835.

——, *The Modern Builder's Guide*, New York, 1853.

Lancaster, Clay, *Old Brooklyn Heights*, Rutland, 1961.

Larrabee, Eric, "Saarinen's Dark Tower," *Harper's Magazine*, December, 1964.

Larrabee, Harold A., "How Ramée Came to Schenectady," *Union College Alumni Monthly*, February, 1937.

——, *Joseph-Jacques Ramée and America's First Unified College Plan*, New York, 1934.

Lynes, Russell, *The Tastemakers*, New York, 1954.

McAllister, Ward, *Society as I Have Found It*, New York, 1890.

McCoy, Garnett, "Visits, Parties and Cats in the Hall: The Tenth Street Studio Building and Its Inmates in the Nineteenth Century," *Journal of the Archives of American Art*, January, 1966.

McKenna, Rosalie Thorne, "James Renwick, Jr., and the Second Empire Style in the United States," *Magazine of Art*, March, 1951.

Mayer, Grace, *Once Upon a City*, New York, 1958.

Millar, Donald, "Quaint Dutch Survival, Jean Hasbrouck House, New Paltz," *Architectural Record*, March, 1926.

Mitchell, Broadus, *Frederick Law Olmsted*, Baltimore, 1924.

A Monograph on the Work of McKim, Mead & White, 4 v., New York, 1925.

Moore, Charles, *Charles Follen McKim*, Boston, 1929.

Morrison, Hugh S., *Early American Architecture*, New York, 1952.

Nevins, Allan, ed., *The Diary of Philip Hone*, New York, 1936.

New York State Council on the Arts, *Architecture Worth Saving in Onondaga County*, Syracuse, 1966.

Newton, Roger H., *Town & Davis: Architects*, New York, 1942.

Olmsted, Frederick L., Jr., and Theodora Kimball, *Frederick Law Olmsted*, 2 v., New York, 1922–28.

Petersen, L. A., *Elisha Graves Otis*, Newcomen Society, New York, 1945.

Phelps-Stokes, Isaac N., *Iconography of Manhattan Island*, 6 v., New York, 1915–18.

Reed, Henry H., and Sophia Duckworth, *Central Park: A History and a Guide*, New York, 1967.

Reynolds, Helen W., *Dutch Houses in the Hudson Valley Before 1776*, New York, 1929.

Riis, Jacob A., *How the Other Half Lives*, New York, 1890.

——, *The Making of an American*, New York, 1901.

Root, Edward W., *Philip Hooker*, New York, 1929.

Schuyler, Montgomery, "The Works of the Late Richard Morris Hunt," *Architectural Record*, October-December, 1896.

——, "The Works of William Appleton Potter," *Architectural Record*, September, 1909.

Shelton, William H., *The Jumel Mansion*, Boston, 1916.

Silver, Nathan, *Lost New York*, Boston, 1967.

Simpson, Sarah H. J., "The Federal Procession in the City of New York," *New-York Historical Society Quarterly*, July, 1925.

Steinman, D. B., *The Builders of the Bridge*, New York, 1945.

Stephens, Ann S., *Fashion and Famine*, New York, 1854.

Stewart, William R., *Grace Church and Old New York*, New York, 1924.

Sturgis, Russell, "A Review of the Work of George B. Post," *Architectural Record*, June, 1898.

——, "The Works of Bruce Price," *Architectural Record*, June, 1899.

——, "The Works of McKim, Mead & White," *Architectural Record*, May, 1895.

Tunnard, Christopher, "Joseph-Jacques Ramée and Union College," *Union Worthies*, Union College, No. 10, 1964.

Upjon, Everard M., *Richard Upjohn: Architect and Churchman*, New York, 1939.

Van Brunt, Henry, *Richard Morris Hunt: A Memorial Address*, Washington, 1896.

Van Pelt, J. V., *A Monograph on the W. K. Vanderbilt House*, New York, 1925.

Van Rensselaer, Marianna G., *Henry Hobson Richardson and His Works*, Boston, 1888.

Weisman, Winston, "Commercial Palaces of New York, 1854–75," *Art Bulletin*, December, 1954.

——, "New York and the Problem of the First Skyscraper," *Journal of the Society of Architectural Historians*, March, 1953.

——, "Slab Buildings," *Architectural Review*, February, 1952.

——, "Towards a New Environment," *Architectural Review*, December, 1950.

Wharton, Edith, *A Backward Glance*, New York, 1934.

White, Alfred T., *Sun-Lighted Tenements: Thirty-five Years Experience as an Owner*, New York, 1912.

White, Lawrence G., *Sketches and Designs by Stanford White*, New York, 1920.

White, Norval, and Elliot Willensky, *AIA Guide to New York City*, New York, 1967.

Wight, Peter B., "Reminiscences of Russell Sturgis," *Architectural Record*, August, 1909.

Wilde, Edward S., "The New York City Hall," *Century Magazine*, April, 1884.

Winthrop, Theodore, *Cecil Dreeme*, New York, 1861.

Wood, Florence, *Memories of William Halsey Wood*, Philadelphia, 1938.

"The Works of Ernest Flagg," *Architectural Record*, April, 1902.

"The Works of Messrs. Carrère & Hastings," *Architectural Record*, January, 1910.

WAYNE ANDREWS

Born in Kenilworth, Illinois, in 1913, Mr. Andrews was educated in the Winnetka public schools, Lawrenceville School, and Harvard College. Later he received his doctorate in American history at Columbia University under the sponsorship of Allan Nevins. From 1948 to 1956 he was Curator of Manuscripts at the New-York Historical Society. From 1956 to 1963 he was an editor at Charles Scribner's Sons. In 1964 he became Archives of American Art Professor at Wayne State University, Detroit.

Mr. Andrews' photographic histories included *Architecture in America* (1960) and *Architecture in Chicago and Mid-America* (1968). He was the author of *The Vanderbilt Legend* (1941), *Battle for Chicago* (1946), *Architecture, Ambition and Americans* (1955), *Germaine: A Portrait of Madame de Staël* (1963), and *Architecture in Michigan* (1967). He was also the editor of *The Best Short Stories of Edith Wharton* (1958), and under the pseudonym Montagu O'Reilly was the author of *Who Has Been Tampering with These Pianos?* He contributed to such publications as *The Architectural Review*, *Town and Country*, *House Beautiful*, *House and Garden*, *Harper's*, *Harper's Bazaar*, *The Saturday Review*, and *The New York Times*. He was also a president of the New York chapter of the Society of Architectural Historians.